# FAITHFUL TO CHRIST

## A Challenge to Truly Live for Christ

## CHARLES H. SPURGEON

We love hearing from our readers. Please contact us at www.anekopress.com/questions-comments with any questions, comments, or suggestions.

*Faithful to Christ* – Charles H. Spurgeon
Revised Edition Copyright © 2019

*Cover Design: J. Martin*
*Crown Illustration: VladisChern/Shutterstock*
*Cover Background: one AND only/Shutterstock*
*Editors: Paul Miller and Ruth Clark*

Printed in the United States of America
Aneko Press

www.anekopress.com

Aneko Press, Life Sentence Publishing, and our logos are trademarks of Life Sentence Publishing, Inc.
203 E. Birch Street
P.O. Box 652
Abbotsford, WI 54405

**RELIGION / Christian Life / Spiritual Growth**

Paperback ISBN: 978-1-62245-653-6
eBook ISBN: 978-1-62245-654-3

10  9  8  7  6  5  4  3

Available where books are sold

# Contents

# Chapter 1

# Pride

There is nothing the human heart falls into as easily as pride, and yet there is no sin that is more frequently, more emphatically, and more eloquently condemned in Scripture.

**Pride is unjustified.** It stands upon the sand, or worse than that, it puts its foot upon the waves of the sea that give way beneath its step – or worse still, it stands upon bubbles that soon must burst beneath its feet. Of all things, pride has the worst foothold. It has no solid rock on earth on which to place itself. We have reasons for almost everything, but we have no reasons for pride. Pride is something that should be unnatural to us, for we have nothing to be proud of.

**Pride is foolish.** It brings no profit with it. There is no wisdom in self-exaltation. Other sins might have some excuse, for people might seem to gain by them. People might make excuses and find temporary worldly benefit in greed, pleasure, and lust, but the person who is proud sells his soul cheaply. He opens wide the floodgates of his heart to let people see how deep the flood within his soul is, but then suddenly it flows out and all is gone; nothing is left. For one puff of empty wind, one word of sweet applause – the soul is gone, and not a drop is left.

In almost every other sin, we gather up the ashes when the fire is gone, but here, what is left? The covetous person has his shining gold, but what does the proud person have? He has less than he would have had without his pride, and he has gained no advantage whatsoever. Pride does not win any crowns. No one, not even the lowest people on earth, honor it. All people look down on the proud person and consider him less than themselves.

**Pride is the most unreasonable thing that can exist.** It feeds upon itself. It will take away its own life, that with its blood it may make a ribbon for its shoulders. It weakens and undermines its own house so that it can build its pinnacles a little higher, and then the whole structure tumbles down. Nothing proves people to be so foolish as pride.

**Pride is inconstant.** It changes its shape. It takes all forms in the world. You can find it in any manner you choose. You can see it in the beggar's rags as well as in the rich man's garments. It dwells with the rich and with the poor. The man without a shoe on his foot may be as proud as if he were riding in a chariot. Pride can be found in every rank of society – among all classes of people. Sometimes it is an Arminian and it talks about the power of the creature. Then it turns Calvinist and boasts of its imagined security, forgetful of the Maker, who alone can keep our faith alive.

Pride can profess any form of religion. It may be a Quaker and wear no collar to its coat. It may be a churchman and worship God in splendid cathedrals. It may be a Dissenter and go to the common meetinghouse. It is one of the most diverse things in the world. It attends all kinds of chapels and churches. No matter where you go, you will see pride. It comes up with us to the house of God. It goes with us to our houses. It is found in business and in leisure, in the streets and everywhere.

Let me hint at one or two forms that it assumes. Sometimes

pride takes a doctrinal shape. It teaches the doctrine of self-sufficiency. It tells us what we can do, and will not admit that we are lost, fallen, debased, and ruined creatures, as we are. It hates divine sovereignty and condemns the doctrine of election.

Then, if it is driven from that, it takes another form. It acknowledges that the doctrine of free grace is true, but does not feel it. It acknowledges that salvation is of the Lord alone, but still it urges people to seek heaven by their own works, even by the deeds of the law. When driven from that, it will persuade people to add something to Christ in the matter of salvation. When that is all torn up and the poor rag of our righteousness (Isaiah 64:6) is all burned, pride will get into the Christian's heart as well as the sinner's. It will flourish under the name of self-sufficiency, teaching the Christian that he is *rich and increased with goods and have need of nothing* (Revelation 3:17). It will tell him that he does not need daily grace, but that past experience will suffice for tomorrow. It tells him that he already knows enough, toils enough, and prays enough.

**Pride has ten thousand shapes.**

Pride will make him forget that he has not yet attained. It will not allow him to press forward to the things that are before, forgetting the things that are behind (Philippians 3:12-14). It enters into his heart and tempts him to set up an independent business for himself – and until the Lord brings about a spiritual bankruptcy, pride will keep him from going to God.

Pride has ten thousand shapes. It is not always that unfriendly and formal gentleman that you picture. It is a vile, creeping, manipulating thing that will twist itself like a serpent into our hearts. It will talk of humility and speak about being dust and ashes. I have known people to talk about their corruption extremely well, pretending to be completely humble, while at the same time they were the proudest reprobates who could be found this side of the gulf of separation.

O my friends! You cannot tell how many shapes pride will assume. Look carefully around you, or you will be deceived by it, and when you think you are entertaining angels, you will find you have been receiving devils unawares (Hebrews 13:2). The true throne of pride everywhere is the heart of man. If we desire, by God's grace, to put down pride, the only way is to begin with the heart.

Now let me tell you a parable in the form of an Eastern story that will set this truth in its proper light. A wise man in the East, called a *dervish*, suddenly came upon a mountain in his wanderings, and he saw beneath his feet a smiling valley, in the midst of which there flowed a river. The sun was shining on the stream, and the water, as it reflected the sunlight, looked pure and beautiful. When he descended, he found that the stream was muddy and that the water was utterly unfit for drinking.

Nearby he saw a young man, a shepherd, who was diligently filtering the water for his flocks. At one moment he poured some water into a pitcher and allowed it to stand. After the dirt had settled, he poured the clean water into a cistern. Then in another place, he would turn aside the current for a little while, letting it ripple over the sand and stones so that the water would be filtered and the impurities removed.

The dervish watched the young man attempting to fill a large cistern with clear water, and he said to him, "My son, why all this toil? What is your purpose in doing all this?"

The young man replied, "Father, I am a shepherd. This water is so filthy that my flock will not drink it, and therefore I am obliged to purify it little by little. I collect enough this way that they can drink, but it is hard work." He then wiped the sweat from his brow, for he was exhausted from his toil.

"It is good that you have worked so hard," said the wise

man, "but do you know that your toil is not well applied? With half the labor you could achieve a better result. I think that the source of this stream must be impure and polluted. Let us take a pilgrimage together and see."

They then walked some miles, climbing their way over many rocks, until they came to a spot where the stream took its rise. When they came near to it, they saw flocks of wild fowls flying away and wild beasts of the earth rushing into the forest. These animals had come to drink, and they had soiled the water with their feet. The two men found an open well that continually flowed, but by reason of these animals that constantly disturbed it, the stream was always murky and muddy.

"My son," said the wise man, "get to work now to protect the fountain and guard the well, which is the source of this stream. When you have done that, if you can keep these wild beasts and fowls away, the stream will flow all pure and clear, and you will no longer have need for your toil."

The young man did so, and as he labored, the wise man said to him, "My son, hear the word of wisdom. If you are wrong, do not seek to correct your outward life, but seek first to get your heart correct, for out of it are the issues of life, and your life will be pure when your heart is pure."

So if you want to get rid of pride, you should not think that you can do so by dressing in a certain way or speaking with pious words, but seek God that He would purify your heart from pride, and then assuredly, if pride is purged from your heart, your life also will be humble. Make the tree good, and the fruit will be good (Matthew 12:33). Make the fountain pure, and the stream will be sweet.

# Chapter 2

# Broken Keys

Faith is necessary to salvation because we are told in Scripture that works cannot save. *For by grace are ye saved through faith and that not of yourselves: it is the gift of God, not of works, lest any man should boast* (Ephesians 2:8-9).

Here is a very familiar story that can be understood by all: One day a minister was going to preach. He climbed a hill on his road. Beneath him lay the villages, sleeping in their beauty, with the cornfields motionless in the sunshine. He did not look at them, though, for his attention was upon a woman standing at her door, and who, upon seeing him, approached with the greatest anxiety, saying, "O sir, do you have any keys with you? I have broken the key of my drawers, and there are some things that I must get immediately."

He said, "I have no keys." She was disappointed, expecting that everyone would have some keys. "But suppose," he said, "I had some keys that would not fit your lock, and therefore you could not get the things you want. Do not distress yourself, but wait until someone else comes up." Wanting to make good use of the occasion, he added, "But have you ever heard of the key of heaven?"

"Ah, yes!" she said. "I have lived long enough, and I have gone to church long enough, to know that if we work hard, get our bread by the sweat of our brow, act well toward our neighbors, behave, as the catechism says, lowly and reverently to all our betters, do our duty in that station of life in which it has pleased God to place us, and say our prayers regularly, we will be saved."

"Ah!" he said. "My good woman, that is a broken key, for you have broken the commandments. You have not fulfilled all your duties. It is a good key, but you have broken it."

"Please, sir," she said, looking frightened and believing that he understood the matter, "tell me what I have left out."

"Why," he said, "the all-important thing – the blood of Jesus Christ. Don't you know it is said in Revelation 3:7 that Jesus holds the key of heaven, and what He opens, no one shuts, and what He shuts, no one opens?" Explaining it to her more fully, he said, "It is Christ, and Christ alone, who can open heaven to you, and not your good works."

"What!" she said. "Are our good works useless, then?"

"No," he answered, "not after faith. If you believe first, you can have as many good works as you please; but if you believe God's Word, you will never trust in your works, for if you trust in them you have spoiled them and they are not good works any longer. Have as many good works as you please, but still put your trust wholly in the Lord Jesus Christ, for if you do not, your key will never unlock heaven's gate."

So, then, we must have true faith, because the old key of works is so broken by us all that we can never enter paradise by it. To be very plain with you, *If we say that we have no sin, we deceive ourselves, and there is no truth in us* (1 John 1:8). If you think that you will enter heaven by your good works, never was there a more deadly delusion, and you will find, at the last great day, that your hopes were worthless. Like dry leaves from the autumn trees, your noblest works will be blown away. They will be kindled into a flame in which you yourselves must suffer forever. Take heed of your good works; get them after faith, but remember – the way to be saved is simply to believe in Jesus Christ.

Without faith it is impossible to be saved and to please God (Hebrews 11:6), because without faith there is no union with Christ. Union with Christ is indispensable to our salvation. If I come before God's throne with my prayers, I will never get them answered unless I bring Christ with me. The Molossians of old, once when they could not get a favor from their king, adopted a striking strategy: they took the king's only son in their arms, fell on their knees, and cried, "O king, for your son's sake, grant our request!"

> Take heed of your good works; get them after faith, but remember – the way to be saved is simply to believe in Jesus Christ.

The king smiled and said, "I deny nothing to those who plead in my son's name."

It is the same way with God. He will deny nothing to the person who comes to Him with Jesus Christ at his side; but if he comes alone, he will be cast away. Union with Christ is, after all, the great point in salvation.

Let me tell you a story to illustrate this. The amazing falls of Niagara have been spoken of in every part of the world, but while they are marvelous to hear of and wonderful to see, they have been very destructive to human life when by accident anyone has been carried down them.

Some years ago, two men, a bargeman and a coal miner, were in a boat and found themselves unable to manage it. It was carried so swiftly down the current that they both were inevitably going to be carried over the falls and dashed to pieces. People on the shore saw them, but were unable to do much for their rescue. At last, however, one man was saved by grasping a rope that someone threw to him. The same instant that the rope came into his hand, a log floated by the other man. The thoughtless and confused bargeman, instead of seizing the rope, laid hold on the log. It was a fatal mistake.

They were both in imminent peril, but the one man was drawn to shore because he had a connection with the people on the land, while the other man, clinging to the log, was carried irresistibly along and was never heard from again. Do you not see that here is a practical illustration? Faith is a connection with Christ. Christ is on the shore, so to speak, holding the rope of faith. If we lay hold of it with the hand of our confidence, He pulls us to shore; but our good works, having no connection with Christ, drift along down the gulf of deadly despair. We can grasp them as tightly as we can, even with hooks of steel, but they cannot help us at all.

# Chapter 3

# Double-Mindedness

Balaam said, *I have sinned* (Numbers 22:34), yet he went on with his sin afterward. One of the strangest characters in the whole world is Balaam. I have often marveled at that man. He seems really in another sense to have come up to the lines of Ralph Erskine:

> To good and evil equal bent,
> I'm both a devil, and a saint.[1]

Balaam did seem to be this way (see Numbers 22-24). At times no one could speak more eloquently and more truthfully, and at other times he exhibited the most loathsome and shameful covetousness that could disgrace human nature.

Look – there is Balaam now. He stands upon the brow of the hill, and there lie the multitudes of Israel at his feet. He is asked to curse them, and he cries, *Why should I curse one whom God has not cursed?* God opens Balaam's eyes and begins to tell him even about the coming of Christ, and Balaam says, *I shall see*

---

1     From the poem "The Believer's Riddle; Or The Mystery of Faith," by the Scottish clergyman Ralph Erskine (1685-1752).

*him, but not now; I shall behold him, but not near by.* And then he winds up his oration by saying, *Let my soul die the death of the righteous, and let my last end be like his!*

You might think that Balaam is a hopeful character, that he will turn out to be a great guy. However, wait until he has come off the brow of the hill, and you will hear him give the most diabolical advice to the king of Moab that it was even possible for Satan himself to suggest. He basically said to the king, "You cannot overthrow these people in battle, for God is with them; try and entice them from their God."

You know how with shameless lusts the people of Moab tried to entice the children of Israel from allegiance to God. So this man, Balaam, seemed to have the voice of an angel at one time, and yet had the very soul of a devil in his heart. He was a terrible character. He was a man of two things, a man who went all the way with two things to a very great extent. I know the Scripture says, *No one can serve two masters* (Matthew 6:24). Now this is often misunderstood. Some read it, "No man can serve *two* masters." Yes, he can; he can serve three or four.

The way to read it is this: "No man can serve two *masters*." They cannot both be masters. He can serve two, but they cannot both be his master. A man can serve two, or twenty, who are not his masters. He can live for twenty different purposes, but he cannot live for more than one master purpose – there can only be one master purpose in his soul.

Balaam labored to serve two masters. It was like the people of whom it was said, *They feared the LORD and served their own gods* (2 Kings 17:33). Or it was like Rufus, who was a loaf of the same leaven. King Rufus painted God on one side of his shield and the devil on the other, and had this motto underneath: "Ready for both; catch who can." There are many such people who are ready for both. They meet a minister, and how pious and holy they are! On the Lord's Day, you would think that they are the most respectable and upright people in the world. They talk in a way that they think is eminently religious. On a weekday, though, if you want to find the greatest reprobates and cheats, they are some of those same people who are so sanctimonious in their piety.

Rest assured that no confession of sin can be genuine unless it is a wholehearted one. It is of no use for you to say, "I have sinned," and then keep on sinning. "I have sinned," you say, and it is a good, fair face you show, but you will go away and willingly commit the same sin!

Some people seem to be born with two characters. When in the library at Trinity College, Cambridge, I noticed a very fine statue of Lord Byron. The librarian said to me, "Stand here, sir."

> It is meaningless and useless for you to say, "I have sinned," unless you mean it from your heart.

I looked, and I said, "What a fine intellectual countenance! What a grand genius he was!"

"Come here," he said, "to the other side."

"Ah, what a demon! There stands the man that could defy the Deity." He seemed to have such a scowl and such a dreadful look on his face, even as Milton would have painted Satan when he said, "Better to reign in hell than serve in heaven." I turned away and said to the librarian, "Do you think the artist designed this?"

"Yes," he said. "He wanted to picture the two characters – the great, the grand, the almost superhuman genius that he possessed, and yet the enormous mass of sin that was in his soul."

There are some people of the same sort. Like Balaam, they would overthrow everything that is contrary to their desires. They could work miracles, but at the same time there is something about them which betrays a horrid character of sin, as great as that which would appear to be their character for righteousness.

Balaam, you know, offered sacrifices to God upon the altar of Baal; that was just the type of character he was.

Many people do the same thing. They offer sacrifices to God on the shrine of this world and wealth. While they will give to the building of a church and donate to the poor, they will at the other door of their office grind the poor for bread and press the very blood out of the widow in order that they may enrich themselves. It is meaningless and useless for you to say, "I have sinned," unless you mean it from your heart. The double-minded person's confession is of no avail.

# Chapter 4

# Labor that Doesn't Satisfy

*But this I say, brothers, the time is short; for the rest, let those that have wives be as though they had none; and those that weep, as though they wept not; and those that rejoice, as though they rejoiced not; and those that buy, as though they possessed not; and those that use this world, as not using it as their own, for the fashion of this world passes away.* (1 Corinthians 7:29-31)

The first act introduces those who have wives. It opens with a wedding. The bride and bridegroom advance to the altar in wedding attire. The bells are ringing. Crowds are cheering at the door, while overflowing joy reigns within. In another scene we observe domestic happiness and prosperity – a loving husband and a happy wife. Further on in the performance, rosy children are climbing on the father's knee. The little toddlers are lisping their mother's name.

"Now," says our friend as he gazes with delight, "this is real and enduring. I know it is. This will satisfy me. I crave for nothing more than this. *Home* is a word as sweet as heaven, and healthy, happy children are as fine a possession as even angels can desire. On this rock I will build all my hope. Just give me this, and I cheerfully renounce the wonderful joys of Christianity."

We whisper in our companion's ear that all this is only a changing scene and it will soon pass away, for time is short, and wife and children are dying creatures. The man laughs at us and says, "Fanatics and enthusiasts may seek eternal joys, but these are enough for me."

He believes that if there is anything permanent in the universe, it is marrying and being given in marriage, educating and bringing up a family, and seeing them all comfortably settled. He is right in valuing the blessing, but wrong in making it his all. Will he see his error before the curtain falls, or will he continue to base the hopes of an immortal spirit upon dying joys? See the green mounds in the cemetery and the headstone with "Here he lies." Alas for thee, poor deluded creature of the world, where is your soul now? Does it console you that the dust of your offspring will mingle with your own ashes? Where do you have a home now? What family do you have now to care for?

The first act is over. Take a breath and say, *This also is vanity* (Ecclesiastes 7:6).

Sadly, the tenor of the drama soon changes! Household joys are linked with household sorrows. *Those that weep* are now before us in the second act. The cloudy and dark days have come. There are parents wringing their hands in grief. A beloved child has died, and they are following its corpse to the tomb.

Soon the merchant suffers a tremendous financial loss. He puts his hand to his aching head and mourns, for he does not know when his troubles will end. The wife is smitten by the hand of death. She lies on her bed, made pale with sickness and exhausted in pain. Her weeping husband is at her side, and then there is another funeral. In the dim distance I see the black horses again and again.

The troubles of mankind are frequent, and sorrow's visits

are not few and far between. Our man of the world is much moved at this second act, foreseeing his own sorrows therein. He weeps, expressing his feelings. He earnestly clutches us and cries, "Surely this is terribly real. You cannot call this a fleeting sorrow or a light affliction. I will forever wring my hands in anguish. The delight of my eyes has been taken from me. I have lost all my joys now. My beloved in whom I trusted has withered like a leaf in autumn before my face. Now I will despair. I will never look up again!"

"I have lost my fortune," says the afflicted merchant, "and distress overwhelms me; this world is indeed a wilderness to me. All its flowers are withered. I would not give a snap of my finger to live now, for everything worth living for is gone!"

Sympathizing deeply with our friend, we nevertheless venture to tell him that to the Christian, these are not killing sorrows, because these trials are so short and produce such lasting good. "Ah!" he says. "You people of faith might talk that way, but I cannot. I tell you these are real things."

Like an English sailor who was watching a play and jumped up on the stage to help a lady in distress, believing that the whole thing was real, so do such people weep and sigh as if they were to mourn forever because some earthly good has been removed. They need to know that the human mourner has never yet explored the depths of sorrow! Oh, that they would escape from those lower depths where immortal spirits weep and wail amid an emphasis of misery! The sorrows of time are trivial indeed when compared with the pains of everlasting punishment.

On the other hand, we consider that *the sufferings of this present time are not worthy to be compared with the coming glory which shall be manifested in us* (Romans 8:18). They are but light afflictions, which are but for a moment (2 Corinthians 4:17), a mere pinprick to the person of faith. Happy is the one whose eyes are open to see that heirs of heaven sorrow not as those who are without hope (1 Thessalonians 4:13). Real joy from above is always with believers, and it is only the shadow of sorrow that falls upon them. Let the curtain drop there. Let us enter into an eternal state, and what and where are these temporary griefs?

Now the third act begins and presents us with a view of *those that rejoice*. It may be that the firstborn son has come of age and there are great festivities. They are eating and drinking in the servants' hall and in the master's banquet chamber. There are high notes of joy and many compliments, and the smiling father is as glad as a man can be. Maybe it is the daughter's wedding, and kind friends implore a thousand blessings on her head while the father smiles and shares the joy. Perhaps it is a gain in business, a successful business venture, or the profits of industry have come flowing in, slowly perhaps, but still surely, and the man is full of rejoicing. He has a house, a home, friends, a successful reputation, and honor, and in the eyes of all who know him, he is happy. Those who do not know him think he has no cares and no sorrows and that his life must be one perpetual feast. They think that surely there can be no spot in his sun, no winter in his year, and no ebb to follow his floods.

Our friend by our side is smiling at this sunny picture. "There," he says, "is that not real? Why, there must be something in that! What more do you want? Only let me get the same, and I will leave the joys of faith, heaven, and immortality to yourselves. These are the things for me. Only let me laugh and have a good time, and you can pray all you want. Fill the bowl high for me; put the roast and the other good food on the table, and let me eat and drink, for tomorrow I die."

If we gently hint to our friend that all this passes away like a vision of the night and that we have learned to look on it as though it were not, he laughs us to scorn and considers us to be crazy, when he is most unreasonable himself. As for ourselves, so far from resting upon the softest couch that earth can give us, we reject its vain delights.

The fourth act of the drama is now before us, and *those that buy* demand our attention. The merchant is neither a mourner nor a man of amusement. In the eyes of certain people who love wealth, he is attending to the one thing needful, the most substantial of all concerns. Feast your eyes here. There are his bags of money; hear how they thump on the table! There are the rolls of bonds, the banker's books, the title deeds of estates, mortgages and securities, and his investments.

He has been successful in life, and he still adheres to business, as he should do. Like a hardworking man, he is still accumulating and piling up his wealth, meanwhile adding field to field and estate to estate, until soon he will possess a whole county. He is now buying a large and very fine house where he intends to spend the remainder of his days, for he is about to retire from business. The lawyer is busy making out the transfer, the sum of money is waiting to be paid, and the whole thing is as good as settled.

"Ah, now," says our friend, who is looking on at the play, "are you going to tell me that this is all a shadow? It is not; there is something very solid and real here, or at least something that will perfectly satisfy me."

We tell him that there may be something that will satisfy *him*, but *our* desires are of a larger span, and nothing but God can fill them. How sad for the one who can find satisfaction in earthly things! It will only be temporary, for when he comes to lie upon his deathbed, he will find his buying and his selling to be poor things with which to stuff a dying pillow. He will find that his gains and acquisitions bring but little comfort to an aching heart, and no peace at all to a conscience exercised with the fear of the wrath to come.

"Ah!" he cries, and sneers sarcastically, putting us aside as not mentally stable. "Let me trade and make a fortune, and that is enough for me; with that I will be well content!" Alas, poor fool, the snow melts not sooner than the joy of wealth, and the smoke of the chimney is as solid as the comfort of riches!

We must not miss the fifth act. See the rich man, our friend who recently got married, the one whom we earlier saw in trouble, and afterwards rejoicing and then prospering in business. He has entered upon a good old age; he has retired, and has now come to *use this world*. The world says he has been a wise man and has done well, for all people will praise you when you do well for yourself.

This man now keeps a full table, a fine garden, excellent horses, and many servants. He has all the comforts that wealth can provide, and as you look around his noble park, gaze at his avenue of fine old trees, or stay a day or two at the family mansion and notice all its luxuries, you hear your friend saying, "Yes, there is something very real here. What do you think of this?"

We hint that the gray hairs of the owner of all these riches indicate that his time is short, and that if this is all he has, he is a very poor man, for he will soon have to leave it, and that his regrets in leaving will make his death more to be pitied than that of a pauper.

Our friend replies, "Ah! You are always talking this way. I tell you that this is not a play. I believe it is all real and substantial, and I am not, by anything you say, made to think that it is unsubstantial and will soon be gone."

O world, you have some fine actors to be able to cheat people so well, or else mortal man is easily fooled, taken in your net like the fishes of the sea. The whole matter is most clearly a show, yet people give their souls to win it. Why, O people of the world, do you do such things? *Why do ye spend money for that which is not bread? and your labour for that which does not satisfy?* (Isaiah 55:2).

# Chapter 5

# The Table of the Reprobate

Take a warning glance at the house of feasting that Satan has built, for just as wisdom has built her house and *hewn out her seven pillars* (Proverbs 9:1), so folly has its temple and its tavern of feasting into which it continually tempts the careless. Look within the banqueting house, and I will show you four tables and the guests who sit at the tables. As you look at those tables, you will see the courses brought in.

At the first table to which I invite your attention, though I plead with you never to sit down and drink at that table, sit the recklessly extravagant. Their table is a mirthful table. It is covered over with a showy crimson, and all the vessels upon it look exceedingly bright and glistening. Many people sit at that table, but they do not know that they are the guests of hell, and that the feast will end in the depths of perdition.

Do you see now the great governor of the feast as he comes in? He has a soft smile upon his face. His garments are not black, but he is girded with a robe of many colors. He has a flattering word on his lip and a tempting charm in the sparkle of his eye. He brings in the cup and says, "Hey, young man, drink some of this. It sparkles in the cup, it moves itself flawlessly. Do you see it? It is the wineglass of *pleasure*."

This is the first cup at the banqueting house of Satan. The young man takes and sips it. At first it is a cautious sip. He only takes a little sip, and then he restrains himself. He does not intend to indulge much in lust; he does not intend to plunge headlong into eternal damnation. There is a flower there on the edge of that cliff. He will reach forward a little and pluck it, but it is not his intention to throw himself from that rugged cliff and kill himself. Not he! He thinks it will be easy to put away the cup after he has tested its flavor! He has no intention to give himself over to its intoxication.

He takes a little sip – but oh, how sweet it is! How it makes his blood tingle within him! *What a fool I was not to have tasted this before!* he thinks. Was ever any joy like this? Could it be thought that our bodies could be capable of such ecstasy as this?

He drinks again. This time he takes a bigger sip, and the wine is hot in his veins. Oh, how blessed is he! What would he not say now in the praise of Bacchus, or Venus, or whatever shape Beelzebub chooses to assume? He becomes a very orator in praise of sin! It is fair, it is pleasant. The deep damnation of lust appears as joyous as the transports of heaven.

He drinks, he drinks, he drinks again, until his brain begins to reel with the intoxication of his sinful delight. This is the first course. Drink, O ye drunkards of Ephraim, and bind the crown of pride about your head, and call us fools because we put your cup from us. Drink with the harlot and eat with the lustful. You might think yourselves wise for doing so, but we know that after these things there comes something worse, *Therefore, their vine is of the vine of Sodom and of the fields of Gomorrah; their grapes are grapes of gall, their clusters are very bitter. Their wine is the poison of dragons and the cruel venom of asps* (Deuteronomy 32:32-33).

*Woe to the crown of pride, to the drunkards of
Ephraim and to the open flower of the beauty of
their glory which is upon the head of the fertile valley of those that are overcome with wine! Behold, the
Lord has a mighty and strong one who as a tempest
of hail and a destroying storm, as a flood of mighty
waters overflowing shall cast down to the earth
with the hand. The crown of pride, the drunkards of
Ephraim, shall be trodden under feet: and the fading flower of the beauty of their glory, which is upon
the head of the fertile valley, shall be as the early
fig, which comes first before the other fruits of the
summer; which when he that looks upon it sees it; as
soon as he has it in his hand, he eats it up. In that
day the LORD of the hosts shall be for a crown of
glory and for a diadem of beauty unto the residue of
his people, and for a spirit of judgment to him that
sits upon the throne of judgment, and for strength to
those that turn the battle to the gate. But they also
have erred through wine, and through strong drink
are out of the way; the priest and the prophet have
erred through strong drink; they are swallowed up of
wine, they are out of the way through strong drink;
they err in vision, they stumble in judgment. For all
tables are full of vomit and filthiness, so that there is
no place clean.* (Isaiah 28:1-8)

Now with a malicious look upon his face, the subtle governor of
the feast rises from his seat. His victim has had enough of the
best wine. He takes away that cup and he brings in another, not
quite so sparkling. Look into the wine; it is not beaded over with
the sparkling bubbles of delight. It is all flat, dull, and tasteless.
It is called the cup of *overindulgence.* The man has had enough

of pleasure, and like a dog he vomits, though like a dog he will return to his vomit yet again (Proverbs 26:11).

*For who shall be the woe?... who shall have redness of eyes? For those that tarry long at the wine* (Proverbs 23:29-30). I am now speaking figuratively of wine, as well as literally. The wine of lust brings the same redness of the eyes; the self-indulgent person soon discovers that all the rounds of pleasure end in being unsatisfied. He says, "What more can I do? I have committed every wickedness that can be imagined, and I have emptied every cup of pleasure. Give me something fresh! I have tried all the entertainment and amusements around. I don't care so much as one single penny for them all. I have gone to every kind of pleasure that I can imagine. It is all over. Pleasure itself grows flat and dull. What am I to do?"

This is the devil's second course: the course of overindulgence – a fitful drowsiness, the result of the previous excess. There are thousands who are drinking of the tasteless cup of self-indulgence every day. Some fresh invention whereby they may kill time, some new discovery whereby they may give a fresh vent to their iniquity, would be a wonderful thing to them. If someone would rise up who could find out for them some new manner of wickedness, some deeper depths in the deeps of the lowest hell of sinful desire, they would bless his name for having given them something fresh to excite them.

That is the devil's second course. Do you see them partaking of it? There are some of you who are drinking deeply of it. You have been made sick by overindulging in lust and desire, the disappointed followers of the fleeting emptiness of pleasure. God knows that if you were to speak your heart out, you would be obliged to say, "There! I have tried pleasure, and I do not find it pleasurable. I have gone around, and just like the blind horse at the mill, I have to go around again. I am spellbound to the sin, but I do not delight in it now as I once did, for all the glory of it is as a fading flower and as the hasty fruit before the summer."

He remains for a while in the rotten sea of his desires, but another scene is opening. The governor of the feast commands another cup to be brought. This time he holds a black goblet, and he presents it with eyes full of hellfire, flashing with fierce damnation. "Drink of that, sir," he says.

The man sips it, jumps back, and shouts, "How could it be that I have come to this!?" You must drink, sir. He who drinks the first cup must drink the second and the third. Drink, even though it might be like fire down your throat! Drink it, even if it is as the lava of Etna in your bowels! Drink! You must drink! He who sins must suffer. He who is a reprobate in his youth must have rottenness in his bones and disease within his loins. He who rebels against the laws of God must reap the harvest in his own body here.

**You can depend upon it that sin carries an infant misery in its bowels.**

Oh! There are some dreadful things that I could tell you about this third course. Satan's house has a front chamber full of everything that is enticing to the eye and enchanting to the sensual taste, but there is a back chamber, and no one knows, no one has seen all of its horrors. There is a secret chamber where he shovels out the creatures whom he himself has destroyed – a chamber beneath whose floor is the blazing of hell, and above whose boards the heat of that horrible pit is felt. It might be a physician's place, rather than mine, to tell of the horrors that many have to suffer as the result of their iniquities.

I will leave that to them, but let me tell the extravagant squanderer that the poverty that he will endure is the result of his sin of extravagant spending and waste. He should also know that the remorse of conscience that will overtake him is not an accidental thing that drops by chance from heaven, but it is the result of his own iniquity. You can depend upon it that sin carries an infant misery in its bowels, and sooner or later it must be delivered of its dreadful child. If we sow the seed, we must reap the harvest. Thus the law of hell's house stands: first, the good wine, then afterwards, that which is worse (John 2:10).

The last course remains to be presented. You strong men who mock at the warning that I would be glad to deliver to you with a brother's voice and an affectionate heart, though with direct language, come here and drink of this last cup. The sinner has at last brought himself to the grave. His hopes and joys were like gold put into a bag full of holes, and they have all vanished – vanished forever, and now he has come to his end. His sins haunt him. His transgressions bewilder him. He is taken like a bull in a net, and how will he escape?

He dies and descends from disease to damnation. Can mere mortal language attempt to tell you the horrors of that last tremendous cup of which the reprobate must drink, and drink forever? Look at it: you cannot see its depths, but cast an eye upon its seething surface. I hear the noise of rushing to and fro, and a sound as of gnashing of teeth and the wailing of despairing souls. *Cast ye the unprofitable slave into the outer darkness; there shall be weeping and gnashing of teeth* (Matthew 25:30).

I look into that cup, and I hear a voice coming up from its depths: *They shall go away into eternal punishment* (Matthew 25:46), *for Tophet is ordained of yesterday for the king of Babylon, it is also prepared; he has deepened and enlarged the pile of her fire and much wood; the breath of the LORD like a stream of brimstone kindles it* (Isaiah 30:33). And what do you say to this last course of Satan? *Who among us shall dwell with the devouring fire?* (Isaiah 33:14).

Degenerate sinner, I urge you in the name of God, move away from this table! Do not be so careless at your cups. Do not be so asleep, secure in the peace that you now enjoy! Death is at the door and swift destruction is at his heels!

As for you who as yet have been restrained by a careful father and the watchfulness of a concerned mother, I implore you to shun the house of sin and foolishness. Let the wise man's words be written on your heart, and remember them in the hour of temptation: *For the lips of the strange woman drop as a honeycomb, and her mouth is smoother than oil, but her end is bitter as wormwood, sharp as a two-edged sword. Her feet go down to death, her steps uphold Sheol. Remove thy way far from her, and do not come near the door of her house* (Proverbs 5:3-5, 8).

# Chapter 6

# The Self-Righteous Guests

D o you see that other table over there in the middle of the palace? There are many relaxed, happy people! Many of you had thought that you never went to the feast of hell at all, but there is a table for you too. It is covered with a bright white tablecloth, and all the vessels on the table are very clean and attractive. The wine does not look like the wine of Gomorrah, but it moves flawlessly, like the wine from the grapes of Eshcol. It seems to have no intoxication in it. It is like the ancient wine that they pressed from the grape into the cup, having in it no deadly poison.

Do you see the people who sit at this table? How self-contented they are! Ask those evil ones who wait at the table, and they will tell you, "This is the table of the self-righteous. The Pharisee sits here. You might know him. He has his phylactery between his eyes and the hem of his garment is made exceedingly broad. He is one of the best of the best who claim to be "Christian" (Matthew 23:5).

"Ah!" Satan says, as he closes the curtain and shuts off the table where the reprobates are feasting. "Be quiet; don't make too much noise, or these sanctimonious hypocrites might realize what company they are in. These self-righteous people are my guests just as much as you are, and I have them quite as safely." So Satan, like an angel of light, brings forth a gilded goblet, looking like the chalice of the table of communion. And what wine is in it? It seems to be the very wine of the sacred Eucharist. It is called the wine of self-satisfaction, and around the brim you can see the bubbles of pride. Look at the swelling froth upon the bowl: *God, I thank thee that I am not as other men are: extortioners, unjust, adulterers, or even as this publican* (Luke 18:11).

You know that cup, my self-deceiving readers. Oh, that you knew the deadly hemlock that is mixed therein! Sin as other people do? Not you; not at all! You are not going to submit yourself to the righteousness of Christ. Why would you need to? You are as good as your neighbors. You think you deserve to go to heaven. You treat everyone fairly and do not lie to them or cheat them. You have never robbed anyone. You help your neighbors. You are as good as other people.

That is the first cup the devil gives. The good wine makes you swell with self-important dignity as its fumes enter your heart and puff it up with a loathsome pride. Yes, I see you sitting in the room that is so cleanly swept and neatly garnished, and I see the crowds of your admirers standing around the table – even many of God's own children, who say, "Oh, that I were half as good as you!"

The very humility of the righteous feeds your pride. Wait awhile, you self-deceived hypocrite; wait awhile, for there is a second course to come. Satan looks at his guests just as satisfied as he looked upon the earlier group of revelers. "Ah!" he says. "I cheated those lively people with the cup of pleasure. Afterward, I gave them the dull cup of self-indulgence, and I have cheated you too. You think that you are all right, but I have deceived you twice. I have made fools of you indeed."

So he brings in a cup that he does not even like to serve all the time. It is called the cup of discontent and restlessness of mind, and there are many who have to drink this after all their self-satisfaction. You who are very good in your own opinion but have no interest in Christ, do you find that when you sit alone and begin to think about your accounts for eternity, they do not come out right somehow – that the balance does not exactly tip to your side after all, as you thought it would? Have you not sometimes found that when you thought you were standing on a rock, there was unsteadiness beneath your feet? You heard the Christian sing boldly:

> Bold shall I stand in that great Day,
> For who aught to my charge shall lay?
> Fully through these absolved I am
> From sin and fear, from guilt and shame.[2]

Then you have said, "Well, I cannot sing that. I have been as good a church member as ever lived. I rarely missed going to church all these years, but I cannot say I have a solid confidence in Jesus and in eternity." You once had a hope of self-satisfaction, but now the second course has come in, and you are not quite so contented.

"Well," says someone else, "I have been to my church, and I have been baptized. I have made a profession of faith, though I was never brought to know the Lord in sincerity and in truth. I once thought it was all well with me, but I now know that I need something that I cannot find." Now comes a shaking in the heart. It is not as delightful as you supposed to build on your own righteousness. Ah! That is the second course.

Wait awhile, and maybe in this world, but certainly in the

---

2    From the hymn, "Jesus, Thy Blood and Righteousness," by Count Nicolaus L. von Zinzendorf (1700-1760).

hour of death, the devil will bring in the third cup – the cup of dismay at the discovery of your lost condition. How many people who have been self-righteous all their lives have, in the end, discovered that the thing on which they had placed their hope had failed them!

I have heard of an army who, being defeated in battle, attempted to make a good retreat. With all their might, the soldiers fled to a certain river where they expected to find a bridge across which they could retreat and find safety. But when they came to the stream, they heard a scream of terror: "The bridge is broken, the bridge is broken!" That cry was in vain, for the multitude hurrying on behind pressed upon those that were ahead, forcing them into the river, until the stream was filled with the bodies of drowned men.

Such must be the fate of the self-righteous. You thought there was a bridge of ceremonies and religion. You believed that baptism, confirmation, and the Lord's Supper made up the solid arches of a bridge of good works and duties. But when you come to die, you will hear the cry, "The bridge is broken, the bridge is broken!"

It will be useless for you to turn around then. Death is close behind you and forces you onward, and you discover what it is to perish through having neglected the great salvation and attempting to save yourself through your own good works. *How will we escape if we neglect so great a salvation?* (Hebrews 2:3 NASB).

This is the last course except for one, and your last course of all, the worst wine, your everlasting portion, must be the same as that of the wicked. As good as you thought yourself to be, inasmuch as you proudly rejected Christ, you must drink the wineglass of the wrath of God – that cup that is full of trembling. *The same shall drink of the wine of the wrath of God, which is poured out without mixture into the cup of his indignation; and he shall be tormented with fire and brimstone in the presence of the holy angels and in the presence of the Lamb; and the smoke of their torment ascends up for ever and ever* (Revelation 14:10-11).

The wicked of the earth will wring out the dregs of that cup and drink them, and you also must drink of it as deeply as they will. *For the cup is in the hand of the LORD, and the wine is red; it is full of mixture; and he pours out of the same; yea, the dregs thereof, shall wring out and swallow up all the wicked of the earth* (Psalm 75:8). Oh, beware in time! Put away your proud looks. *Humble yourselves, therefore, under the mighty hand of God* (1 Peter 5:6). *Believe on the Lord Jesus Christ, and thou shalt be saved* (Acts 16:31).

# Chapter 7

# Drunk with the World

So far, you have escaped the lash, but there is a third table, crowded with most honorable guests. I believe there have been more princes and kings, mayors and councilmen, and important businessmen sitting at this table than at any other. It is called the table of worldliness.

"I don't agree!" someone says. "I dislike the reprobate. Consider my oldest son. I've been hard at work saving up money all my life, and there's that young fellow – he will not stick to business. He has become a real reprobate. I am very glad the minister spoke so directly about that. As for me – there now! I don't care about your self-righteous people a single bit. It doesn't matter to me at all. I don't care at all about Christianity. I want to know whether the stock prices rise or fall or whether there is an opportunity of making a good business deal, but that's about all I care for."

Ah, worldly one! I have read about a friend of yours who was clothed in scarlet and fine linen and dined lavishly every day (Luke 16:19). Do you remember what happened to him? You should remember it, for the same end awaits yourself. How his feast ended will be how yours ends. If your god is this world, you will find your way full of bitterness.

Look now at that table of the worldly man, the mere person of this world who lives for gain. Satan brings him a flowing cup. "There, young man," he says. "You are starting out in business. You do not need to care about the conventionalities of honesty or about the ordinary old-fashioned thoughts about the Christian religion. Instead, get rich as quickly as you can. Get money, get money. Get it honestly if you can, but if not, get it anyway," says the devil.

He puts down a tankard and says, "There is a foaming drink for you."

"Yes," says the young man, "I have abundance now. My hopes are indeed realized."

> "Get money, get money. Get it honestly if you can, but if not, get it anyway," says the devil.

Here, then, you see the first and best wine of the worldly one's feast, and many of you are tempted to envy this man. "Oh, that I had such a future in business!" someone says. "I am not half as sharp as he is. I could not deal as he does. My beliefs would not let me; but how fast he gets rich! Oh, that I could prosper as he does!"

Come, my brother, do not judge before the time. There is a second course to come – the thick and nauseous drink of worry and discontent. The man has got his money, but those who want to be rich fall into temptation and a snare. Wealth ill-gotten, ill-used, or hoarded brings a poison with it that does not harm the gold and silver, but poisons the man's heart; and a poisoned heart is one of the most awful things a person can have.

Ah! See this person who loves money, and notice the care that sits upon his heart. There is a poor old woman who lives near his home. She has but a small amount of money to live on each week, but she says, "Bless the Lord, I have enough!" She never asks how she is to live or how she is to die or how she is to be buried, but she sleeps sweetly on the pillow of contentment and faith; and here is this poor fool with untold gold, but he is miserable because he happened to drop a quarter as he walked along the streets, or because a friend compelled him to give an extra donation to a charity, or maybe he groans because he thinks he needs a new coat.

After this comes greed. Many have had to drink of that cup. May God save us from its fiery drops! A great American preacher has said:

> Covetousness breeds misery. The sight of houses better than our own, of clothing beyond our means, of jewels costlier than we may wear, of expensive vehicles, and rare curiosities beyond our reach – these hatch the viper brood of covetous thoughts, vexing the poor who would be rich, and tormenting the rich who would be richer. The covetous man longs to see pleasure, is sad in the presence of cheerfulness, and the joy of the world is his sorrow because all the happiness of others is not his. I do not wonder that God abhors him. He inspects his heart as he would a cave full of noisome birds or a nest of rattling reptiles, and loathes the sight of its crawling tenants. To the covetous man, life is a nightmare, and God lets him wrestle with it as best as he can. Riches might build its palace on such a heart, and Pleasure might bring all its revelry there. Honor all its garlands – it would be like pleasures in a sepulcher and garlands on a tomb.[3]

When a man becomes full of greed, all he has is nothing to him. "More, more, more!" he says, like some poor creatures

---

3   This is a quote from Henry Ward Beecher (1813-1887) from his book *Addresses to Young Men*.

with a terrible fever who cry, "Drink, drink, drink!" and you give them drink, but after they have it, their thirst increases. *The horseleach has two daughters, which are called, Give, give. There are three things that are never satisfied, yea, four things say not, It is enough: Sheol; and the barren womb; the earth that is not filled with water; and the fire that never says, It is enough* (Proverbs 30:15-16).

This greed and materialism is a raving madness that wants to grasp the world in its arms, and yet despises the plenty it already has. This is a curse of which many have died. Some have died with the bag of gold in their hands and with misery upon their brow because they could not take it with them into their coffin and could not carry it into another world.

Then there comes the next course. Richard Baxter and those powerful old preachers used to picture the miser and the man who lived only to make money as being in the middle of hell. They imagined Mammon pouring melted gold down their throat. "There," say the mocking devils, "this is what you wanted. You have it now. Drink, drink, drink!" and the molten gold is poured down. I will not, however, indulge in any such dreadful imaginations, but this much I know: he who lives to himself here must perish. He who sets his affections upon the things of earth has not dug deep; he has built his house upon the sand. When the rain descends and the floods come, his house will fall down, and great must be the fall thereof. *Every one that hears these words of mine and does not do them shall be likened unto a foolish man, who built his house upon the sand; and the rain descended, and the rivers came, and the winds blew and beat upon that house, and it fell; and great was the fall of it* (Matthew 7:26-27).

It is the best wine first, however. It is the respectable person. He is respectable and respected, and everybody honors him. Afterward, though, comes that which is worst, when depravity has reduced his wealth and covetousness has clouded his brain. It is sure to come if ever you give yourself up to worldliness.

The fourth table is set in a very secluded corner in a very private part of Satan's palace. There the table is set for secret sinners, and there the old rule is observed. At that table, in a room well darkened, I see a young man sitting, and Satan is doing the serving, stepping in so noiselessly that no one can hear him. He brings in the first cup, and oh, how sweet it is! It is the cup of secret sin. *Stolen waters are sweet, and bread eaten in secret is pleasant* (Proverbs 9:17). How sweet that morsel is, eaten all alone! Was there ever one that rolled so delicately under the tongue?

That is the first, and after that he brings in another – the wine of an unquiet conscience. The man's eyes are opened. He says, "What have I done? What have I been doing?" cries this Achan. "In the first cup you brought me, I saw a sparkling wedge of gold and a fine Babylonish garment, and I thought, 'Oh, I must have that.' Now, though, my thought is, 'What can I do to hide this? Where can I put it? I must dig. I must dig as deep as hell before I can hide it, for I am sure that it will be discovered.'" *When I saw among the spoils a goodly Babylonish garment and two hundred shekels of silver and a wedge of gold of fifty shekels weight, then I coveted them and took them; and, behold, they are hid in the earth in the midst of my tent, and the silver under it* (Joshua 7:21).

The grim governor of the feast is bringing in a massive bowl filled with a black mixture. The secret sinner drinks and is confounded. He fears his sin will find him out. *Be sure your sin will catch up with you* (Numbers 32:23). He has no peace, no happiness, and he is full of uneasy fear. He is afraid that he will be detected. He dreams at night that there is someone after him. There is a voice whispering in his ear, telling him, "I know all about it; I will tell it." He thinks, perhaps, that the sin that he has committed in secret will be made known to his friends, and then his father will know it and his mother will find out.

For such a person there is no rest. He is always in dread of being caught. He is like the debtor I read of who owed a great deal of money and was afraid that the bailiffs were after him. One day he got his sleeve caught on top of a fence, and he said, "Let me go. I'm in a hurry. I will pay you tomorrow," imagining that someone was grabbing hold of him. Such is the position in which the man places himself by partaking of the hidden things of dishonesty and sin. He finds no rest for the sole of his foot because he is afraid of being caught. At last your sin is made known. It is the last cup. It often happens while you are on earth, for you can *be sure your sin will catch up with you*, and it will generally find you out here.

What frightful exhibitions are to be seen in our courts of law from people who got caught in their sin and have been made to drink that last fateful drink of being found out! The man who presided at religious meetings, the man who was honored as a saint, is at last unmasked. And what does the judge say? What does the world say about him? He is a joke, a reproach, and a rebuke everywhere.

However, suppose he would be so crafty that he passes through life without his sin being publicly discovered (although I think that is almost impossible). What a cup he must drink when he stands at last before the judgment seat of God! "Bring him forth, jailor! Dread keeper of the dungeon of hell, lead the prisoner out!"

He comes! The whole world is assembled. "Stand up! Did you not make a profession of faith? Did not everybody think that you were a Christian?" He is speechless, but there are many in that vast crowd who cry, "We thought he was." The book is opened and his deeds are read. Transgression after transgression are all laid bare. Do you hear that hiss? The righteous, moved to indignation, are lifting up their voices against the person who deceived them and dwelt among them as a wolf in sheep's clothing.

Oh, how fearful it must be to bear the scorn of the universe! The good can bear the scorn of the wicked, but for the wicked to bear the shame and everlasting contempt that righteous indignation will heap upon them will be one of the most frightful things, next to the eternal endurance of the wrath of the Most High, which, I need not add, is the last cup of the devil's terrible feast with which the secret sinner must be filled forever and ever.

# Chapter 8

# Going through the Fire

See iniquity raging on every side. Its flames are fanned by every wind of our culture. New victims are constantly being drawn in. It spreads to every class of people. Neither the palace nor the shack is safe. Neither the lofty skyscraper nor the graceful church provides safety. Iniquity, whose contagion is as fearful as fire, spreads and preys upon all things that are simple and common. Things useful and things sacred are not exempt.

We must walk through the fire. We who are God's witnesses must stand in its very midst to pour the streams of living water upon the burning fuel, and if we are not able to quench it, at least we must strive to prevent its spread.

I see before my mind's eye the blackened skeletons of hundreds of fine professions of faith. Multitudes – multitudes have perished in the valley of temptation, who once, to all human judgment, had been on the way to heaven and had made a show in the flesh. How many, too, have fallen under the attacks of Satan! This is a fire that does burn.

Many people have said, "I will be a pilgrim," but they met Apollyon on the road, and they have turned back.[4] Many people

---

4    This is a reference to John Bunyan's *The Pilgrim's Progress*, available from Aneko Press.

have put on the armor, but have soon given up the battle. They have put their hands to the plow, but looked back. *Jesus said unto him, No one having put his hand to the plough and looking back is fit for the kingdom of God* (Luke 9:62).

There are more pillars of salt than one. If Lot's wife were a solitary specimen, it would not be so bad, but there have been tens of thousands who, like her, have looked back to the plains of Sodom, and, like her, as they are in their spirit, have stood forever as they were – lost souls. We should not look upon our dangers with contempt. They are dangers. They are trials. We should look upon our temptations as fires – oh, they are fires! If you think they are not fires, you are mistaken. If you enter, then, in your own strength, saying, "Oh, I could handle them," you will find that they are real fires, which, with forked tongues, will lick up your blood and consume it in an instant if you have no better safeguard than your own human power.

*When thou dost walk through the fire, thou shalt not be burned; neither shall the flame kindle upon thee* (Isaiah 43:2). Dr. Alexander, an eminent and most admirable American commentator, says there appears to be some mistake in the translation, because he thinks the two sentences are an anticlimax. *Thou shalt not be burned*, and then follows, *neither shall the flame kindle upon thee*. It strikes me, however, that in the second clause we have the higher gradation of a climax. *Thou shalt not be burned* to the destruction of your life, nor even scorched to give you the most superficial injury, for the flames shall not *kindle upon thee*.

Just as when the three holy young men came out of the fiery furnace, it is said that the fire had no power upon their bodies, not a hair of their head was singed, their outer garments looked the same, and they did not smell at all like smoke or fire (Daniel 3:27). So the text seems to me to teach that the Christian church, under all its trials, has not been consumed;

but more than that, it has not lost anything by its trials. The Lord's church has never been destroyed by her persecutors and her trials. They have thought they crushed her, but she still lives. They had imagined that they had taken away her life, but she sprang up more vigorous than before.

I suppose there is not a nation out of which Christ's church has ever been completely driven. Even Spain, which seemed to have accomplished it at last by the most persevering barbarities, still finds a few believers to be a thorn in the side of her bigotry. As for our own denomination, in the very country where, by the most horrible massacres, it was believed that the sect of Anabaptists had been utterly extinguished, Mr. Oncken[5] became the means of reviving it, so that throughout Germany, and in parts of Denmark, Prussia, Poland, and even Russia itself, we had sprung up into a new, vigorous, and even wonderful existence. In Sweden, where, under a Lutheran government, the most persecuting edicts have been passed against us, we have been astonished to find churches suddenly spring up, for the truth has in it a living seed that is not to be destroyed.

Not only does the church not lose her existence, but she also does not lose anything at all. The church has never lost her numbers. Persecutions have winnowed her and driven away the chaff, but not one grain of wheat has been taken away from the heap. No, not even in visible fellowship has the church been decreased by persecution. She is like Israel in Egypt: the more they were afflicted, the more they multiplied (Exodus 1:12).

If a bishop was put to death, ten young men came the next morning before the Roman officer and offered themselves to die, having that very night been baptized on account of the dead bishop, having made their confession of faith that they might occupy his position. "I will fill up the vacancy in the church, and then die as he did." If a woman was strangled or tortured

---

5    Johann Gerhard Oncken (1800-1884) was a German Baptist preacher known as the "Father of German Baptists" and the "Apostle of European Baptists."

publicly, twenty women appeared the next day, willing to suffer as she suffered that they might honor Christ.

Did the Church of Rome in more recent times burn one of our glorious reformers – John Huss – yet did not Martin Luther come forward as if the ashes of Huss had begotten Luther? When John Wycliffe passed away, did not the very fact of Wycliffe being persecuted help to spread his doctrines? Were there not found hundreds of young men who in every market town in England read the Lollards' Scriptures and proclaimed the Lollards' faith?[6]

You can depend upon it, and it will always remain true: give a dog a bad name, and you hang him; give a Christian a bad name, and you honor him. Just give to any Christian some unkind name, and before long a Christian denomination will take that name to itself and it will become a title of honor.

When George Fox was called "Quaker," it was a strange name – one to laugh at; but those men of God who followed him called themselves Quakers too, and so it lost its reproach. They called the followers of Whitefield and Wesley Methodists; they took the title of Methodists, and it became a respectful designation.

When many of our Baptist forefathers, persecuted in England, went over to America to find shelter, they imagined that among the Puritans they would have a perfect rest, but Puritan liberty of conscience meant the right and liberty to think as they did, but no toleration for those who differed. The Puritans of New England, as soon as a Baptist made his appearance among them, persecuted him with as little misgivings as the Episcopalians had the Puritans. No sooner was there a Baptist than he was hunted down and brought before his own Christian brethren. Note that he was brought up for a fine, imprisonment,

---

6    The Lollards were a group of Christians who followed the teachings of John Wycliffe. The Roman Catholic Church called Wycliffe's disciples "Lollards," from the Latin word for "tare," as in the wheat and the tares.

confiscation, and banishment before the very men who had themselves suffered persecution.

What was the effect of this? The effect has been that in America, where we were persecuted, we are the largest body of Christians. Where the fire burned the most furiously, there the good old Calvinistic doctrine was taught and the Baptist became more decidedly a Baptist than anywhere else, with the most purity and the least dross. Nor, by all the trials and persecutions that have been laid upon us, have we ever lost the firmness of our grip upon the fundamen-

> Upon the entire church, in the end, there will not be even the smell of fire.

tal doctrine for which our forefathers stained the baptismal pool with blood – and we never will.

Upon the entire church, in the end, there will not be even the smell of fire. I see her come out of the furnace. I see her advance up the hill toward her final glory with her Lord and Master, and the angels look at her garments. They are not tattered. No – the fangs of her enemies have not been able to make a single tear in them. They draw near to her; they look upon her flowing hair and see that it is not crisp from the heat. They look at her feet, and although she has been made to walk upon the hot coals, her feet are not blistered. Her eyes have not been dried up by the furiousness of the seven-times-heated flame (Daniel 3:19). She has been made more beautiful, more lovely, more glorious by the fires, but she has not been hurt, nor can she be.

Turn, then, to the individual Christian, and remember that the promise is just as firm and steadfast for each believer. Christian, if you are truly a child of God, your trials cannot destroy you. What is better still, you cannot lose anything by them. You may seem to lose for today, but when the account comes to be settled, you will not be found to have lost at all due to all the temptations of all the world or all the attacks of

Satan that you have endured. On the contrary, you will have wondrously gained. Your trials, having worked patience and experience, will make you rich. Your temptations, having taught you your weakness and shown you where your strength lies, will make you strong. *We even glory in the tribulations, knowing that the tribulation works patience; and patience, experience; and experience, hope; and the hope shall not be ashamed, because the love of God is poured out in our hearts by the Holy Spirit which is given unto us* (Romans 5:3-5).

There is a brother who has had wave upon wave of affliction. Everything goes against him. He is an upright, honest, industrious merchant, yet no matter what he does, his resources waste away like snow before the sun. It appears that for every ship of his, the wind blows the wrong way, and where others win in a business venture, he loses everything.

> Sees every day new straits attend,
> And wonders where the scene will end.[7]

When I spoke of walking through the fire, he said, "Ah! That is what I have been doing. I have been walking through it these months. Only to God and my own soul alone is it known how hot the furnace is."

Brother, take this text home to your heart: *When thou dost walk through the fire, thou shalt not be burned.* When your troubles are all over, you will still be left standing, and what is more, *neither shall the flame kindle upon thee.* When the winding-up time comes, you will not have lost. While you think you have lost much, you will find when you read Scripture that you only lost shadows. Your substance was always safe, being laid up in Christ's keeping in heaven. You will see that these trials

---

7    This is from the hymn "Thus Far My God Hath Led Me On" by John Fawcett (1740-1817).

of yours were the best things that could have happened to you. The day will come when you will say with David, *I will sing of mercy and judgment* (Psalm 101:1), and *Before I was humbled, I went into error, but now I keep thy spoken word* (Psalm 119:67).

Maybe there is some young woman – and the case I am about to paint is a very common one – sadly, too common in this city. You love the Savior, my sister, but you are very poor, and you have to earn your living by difficult means. When the sun rises in the morning, you are ready with that needle in your hand,

> Sewing at once with a double thread;
> A shroud as well as a shirt.[8]

All day long you scarcely have time to rest for meals, and in the evening, when your fingers are worn and your eyes are heavy, you will have need to refrain from sleep because the pay is so small that you can barely live upon it.

We know hundreds like this who always bring forth our compassion because they work so hard for such little wages. Maybe your mother is dead and your father does not care about you. Maybe he is a drunkard and you would be sorry to meet him in the street. You have no helper, no friends. You do not want to tell anybody your troubles. You would not want to accept anything if charity would be offered to you.

You think it is the most difficult thing of all to be tempted as you are. The path to the road to plenty, and in some degree to delight, seems open to you by theft or some other sin. But you have said, "No, no!" and you have loathed the temptation. You have stood firm on what is right. I know how year after year some of you have fought with temptation and struggled on when sometimes you were nearly starved, but you would not do this great wickedness against God. You think, with Joseph,

---

8    This is from the poem "Song of the Shirt" by Thomas Hood (1799-1845).

*How then can I do this great wickedness and sin against God?*
(Genesis 39:9).

My sister, I pray that you will take the encouragement of
Scripture to strengthen you for the future battles. You have been
going through the fires, but you are not consumed yet, and I
thank God that the smell of fire has not passed upon your garments. Hold on, my sister, hold on, through all the sorrow that
you have and through all the bitterness that is heavy enough to
crush your spirit. Hold on, for your Master sees you. He will
encourage and strengthen you and make you more than a con-
queror through it all in the end. *Blessed are those that mourn,
for they shall be comforted* (Matthew 5:4).

How cruel sometimes worldly young men are to Christian
young men! Cruel – for when there are a dozen men of the world
and only one Christian, they consider it to be honorable for the
dozen to attack the one. Twelve big, tall fellows will sometimes
think it is a fun game to shove around some younger boy and
make sport and mockery of him. There is honor, it is said,
among thieves, but there seems to be no honor at all among
the worldly when they meet a young Christian.

Well, young man, you have withstood it. You have said, "I
will hold my tongue and won't say a word," even though your
heart was hot within you, and while you were musing, the fire
burned (Psalm 39:3). Remember, the anvil does not get broken
even if you keep on striking it, but it breaks all the hammers.
You must do the same. Just hold on, and these fires will not
consume you. If the fire should burn up your piety, it would
only prove that your piety was not worth having. If you cannot
stand a few jokes and jeers, then you are not built together in
that habitation of God that He has made fireproof.

Endure to the end, and you will find that this difficult situation, this severe discipline, did you much good and made you
a better man than you ever would have been if you had been

gently rocked on the lap of piety and kept from the battle. Later in your life, your high and eminent post of usefulness might indeed be because of the severe and harsh discipline to which you were put in your younger days. *It is good for the man if he bears the yoke from his youth* (Lamentations 3:27).

Maybe I am speaking to someone who has met with opposition from his own ungodly relatives. Remember how Jesus said, *I am come to cast fire into the earth; and what do I desire, except that it be kindled? For from now on there shall be five in one house divided: three against two and two against three* (Luke 12:49, 52).

Perhaps your father has threatened you, or what is more bitter still, maybe your husband has threatened to leave you. Now indeed you are walking through the fires. He complains about your godliness, mocks everything you love, and does his best by cruelty to break your heart. My dear sister in Christ, you will not be burned by the fire. If grace is in your heart, the devil cannot drive it out, much less can your husband drive it out. If the Lord has called you by His grace, all the people on earth and all the demons in hell cannot reverse the calling. You will find in the end that you have not suffered any loss. The flame has not kindled upon you. You will go through the fire and thank God for it. From a deathbed, or at least through the gates of paradise, you will look back upon the dark path of the way and say that it was well. "It was good for me that I had to carry that cross, and now I am permitted to wear this crown."

> If grace is in your heart, the devil cannot drive it out.

# Chapter 9

# Laziness

You cannot be idle and have Christ's precious communion. Jesus walks quickly, and when His people want to talk with Him, they must travel quickly too, or else they will soon lose His company. Christ, my Master, *went about doing good* (Acts 10:38), and if you want to walk with Him, you must go about with the same mission.

The almighty lover of souls is not inclined to keep company with idle people. I find in Scripture that most of the great appearances that were made to eminent saints were made when they were busy. Moses kept his father-in-law's flock when he saw the burning bush. Joshua was going round about the city of Jericho when he met the angel of the Lord. Jacob was in prayer when the angel of God appeared to him. Gideon was threshing and Elisha was plowing when the Lord called them. Matthew was in the receipt of customs when he was called to follow Jesus. James and John were fishing.

The manna that the children of Israel kept until morning bred worms and stank. Idle grace would soon become active corruption. Moreover, laziness hardens the conscience. It is one of the irons with which the heart is seared. Abimelech hired vain and light persons to promote his cause (Judges 9:4), and the Prince of Darkness does the same.

Oh friends, it is a sad thing to rust the edge off from one's mind and to lose keenness of moral perception, but sloth will surely do this for us. David felt the power of sloth to weaken. He was losing the force of his conscience and was ready for anything. The worst is near at hand. He walked upon the housetop and saw the object that excited his lust. He sent for the woman, and the deed was done. It led to another crime. He tempted Uriah, and that led to murder, as Uriah was put to death. David then took Uriah's wife. Ah, David, David! *How are the valiant fallen!* (2 Samuel 1:27). How has the prince of Israel fallen and has become like the vile fellows who riot in the evening! From this day forth, his sunshine turns to clouds, his peace gives place to suffering, and he goes to his grave an afflicted and troubled man who, though he could say, God *has made an everlasting covenant with me,* yet had to precede it with that very significant sentence, *shall not my house be so with God* (2 Samuel 23:5).

Is there anyone among the Lord's people who would *[crucify] again for themselves the Son of God and putting him to an open shame* (Hebrews 6:6)? Is there any who would want to sell their Master, with Judas, or turn aside from Christ, with Demas? It is easy to accomplish. Oh, you say you could not do it. *Now,* perhaps, you could not, but get slothful, do not fight the Lord's battles, and it will become not only easy for you to sin, but you will surely also become its victim.

Oh, how Satan delights to make God's people fall into sin, for then he does, as it were, thrust another nail into the bloody hand of Christ! It is then that he stains the fine white linen of Christ's own garment. It is then that he boasts that he has gotten a victory over the Lord Jesus and has led one of the Master's servants captive at his will! Oh, if we do not want to make hell ring with satanic laughter and make the men of God weep because the cedars of Lebanon are cut down, let us watch unto prayer and be diligent in our Master's business, *fervent in the Spirit, serving the Lord* (Romans 12:11).

David was saved. I only speak to you who are saved, and I beg and urge you to take notice of David's fall, and of the idleness that was at the beginning of it, as a warning to yourselves. *Some* temptations come to the industrious, but *all* temptations attack the idle. Notice the invention used by country people to catch wasps. They will put a little sweet liquid into a long and narrow-necked vial. The do-nothing wasp comes by, smells the sweet liquid, plunges in, and is drowned. But the bee comes by, and if it does stop for a moment to smell, it does not enter, because it has honey of its own to make. The bee is too busy in the work of the commonwealth to indulge herself with the tempting sweets.

> Idle Christians are not tempted by the devil so much as they tempt the devil to tempt them.

Richard Greenham, a Puritan clergyman, was once waited upon by a woman who said that she was often tempted to sin. Upon asking about her way of life, he found that she had little to do, and Greenham said, "That is the secret of your being so much tempted. Sister, if you are very busy, Satan may tempt you, but he will not easily prevail, and he will soon give up the attempt."

Idle Christians are not tempted by the devil so much as they tempt the devil to tempt them. Idleness opens the door of the heart and asks Satan to come in, but if we are kept busy from morning until night, if Satan does get in, he must break through the door. Under sovereign grace, and next to faith, there is no better shield against temptation than being *not slothful in earnest care, but fervent in the Spirit, serving the Lord* (Romans 12:11).

Let me remind those who are doing little for Christ that

you were not always as cold as you are now. There was a time with David when the sound of the trumpet of war would have stirred his blood and he would have been eager for the battle. There was a day when the very sight of Israel assembled in formation would have made David bold as a lion. Oh, it is a sad thing to see the lion changed like this! God's hero stays at home with the women!

There was a time when you would have gone over hedge and ditch to hear a sermon, and did not mind standing in the aisles; but now the sermons are tiresome to some of you, although you have soft cushions to sit upon. It used to be that if there was a neighborhood prayer meeting or a revival meeting, you were there. Ah, you say, that was wildfire. Blessed wildfire! May the Lord give you the wildfire back again, for even if it was wildfire, that is better than no fire at all. It is better to be called a fanatic than to deserve to be called a drone in Christ's hive.

# Chapter 10

# Faith

A naval officer tells the following remarkable story concerning the siege of Copenhagen under Lord Nelson. An officer in the fleet says, "I was particularly impressed with something that I saw three or four days after the terrible bombardment of that place. For several nights before the surrender, the darkness was ushered in with a tremendous roar of guns and mortars, accompanied by the whizzing of those destructive and burning engines of warfare – Congreve rockets. The dreadful effects were soon visible in the brilliant lights throughout the city. The blazing houses of the rich and the burning cottages of the poor illuminated the heavens. The wide-spreading flames, reflecting on the water, showed a forest of ships assembled around the city ready for its destruction. This work of conflagration went on for several nights, but the Danes at last surrendered.

"Upon walking a few days later among the ruins, which consisted of the cottages of the poor, the houses of the rich, manufacturing buildings, lofty steeples, and humble meeting-houses, I noticed, amid this barren field of desolation, a solitary house unharmed. Everything around it was a burnt mass, but this alone had been untouched by the fire, a monument of mercy. 'Whose house is that?' I asked. 'That,' said the interpreter, 'belongs to a Quaker. He would neither fight nor leave his house, but remained in prayer with his family during the whole bombardment.' Surely, thought I, it *is* well with the righteous. God *has* been a shield to you in battle, a wall of fire round about you, and a very present help in time of need."

That story might seem to be an invention of mine, but it happens to be as authentic a piece of history as any that can be found.

There is another somewhat similar story told of a Danish war. "Soon after the surrender of Copenhagen to the English, in the year 1807, detachments of soldiers were, for a time, stationed in the surrounding villages. It happened one day that three soldiers, belonging to a Highland regiment, were set to search for food among the neighboring farmhouses. They went to several, but found them stripped and deserted.

"At length they came to a large garden, or orchard, full of apple trees, bending under the weight of fruit. They entered by a gate and followed a path that brought them to a fine-looking farmhouse. Everything outside the house seemed to tell of quietness and security, but as they entered by the front door, the lady of the house and her children ran screaming out by the back. The interior of the house presented an appearance of order and comfort superior to what might be expected from people in that station and from the habits of the country.

"A watch hung by the side of the fireplace, and a neat bookcase, well-filled, attracted the attention of the oldest soldier. He took down a book. It was written in a language unknown to him, but the name of Jesus Christ was legible on every page. At this moment, the owner of the house entered by the door through which his wife and children had just fled. One of the soldiers, by threatening signs, demanded provisions. The man stood firm and undaunted, and he shook his head. The soldier who held the book approached him, and pointing to the name of Jesus Christ, laid his hand upon his heart and looked up to heaven. Instantly the farmer grasped his hand, shook it passionately, and then ran out of the room. He soon returned with his wife and children, loaded with milk, eggs, bacon, etc., which were freely given. When money was offered in return, it was at first refused, but as two of the soldiers were pious men, they, much to the displeasure of their companion, insisted upon paying for all they received.

"As they were leaving, the pious soldiers let the farmer know that it would be beneficial for him to hide his watch, but by the most expressive signs, he made them understand that he feared no evil, for his trust was in God, and that although his neighbors on their right and on their left had fled from their houses, and had lost what they could not remove due to the groups of soldiers foraging, not a hair of his head had been injured, nor had he even lost an apple from his trees."

The man knew that *all those that take the sword shall perish by the sword* (Matthew 26:52), so he just tried the faith principle, and God, in whom he put complete confidence, would not let him be injured.

It was an extraordinary thing that in the massacre of the Protestants in Ireland, a long time ago, there were thousands of Quakers in the country, and only two of them were killed – and those two had no faith in their own principles. One of them ran away and hid himself, and the other kept arms in his house. The others, unarmed, walked amid infuriated soldiers, both Roman Catholics and Protestants, and were never touched, because they were strong in the strength of Israel's God. They had put their sword into its sheath, knowing that to war against another cannot be right, since Christ has said, *Resist not with evil, but whosoever shall smite thee on thy right cheek, turn to him the other also* (Matthew 5:39). They knew that Jesus had said to be kind, not only to the thankful, but also *unto the unthankful and to the evil* (Luke 6:35), and to *Love your enemies, bless those that curse you, do good to those that hate you, and pray for those who speak evil about you, and persecute you* (Matthew 5:44).

We are ashamed to do that. We do not like it. We are afraid to trust God, and until we do, we will not know the majesty of faith nor prove the power of God for our protection. *My soul, rest thou only in God, for my hope is from him* (Psalm 62:5).

# Chapter 11

# Awaken, Oh Sleeper!

The sleep of the body is the gift of God. So said Homer of old, when he described it as descending from the clouds and resting on the tents of the warriors around old Troy. So sang Virgil when he spoke of Palinurus falling asleep upon the bow of the ship. Sleep is the gift of God. We think that we lay our heads upon our pillows, put our bodies in a peaceful posture, and then we naturally and necessarily sleep. But it is not so.

Sleep is the gift of God. Not one person would close his eyes if God did not put His fingers on his eyelids. Not one person would fall asleep if the Almighty did not send a soft and calm influence over his body that lulled his thoughts into dormancy, making him enter into that blissful state of rest that we call sleep. True, there are some narcotics whereby people can poison themselves nearly to death and then call it sleep, but the sleep of the healthy body is the gift of God.

The Lord of love bestows it. His tenderness rocks the cradle for us every night. His kindness draws the curtain of darkness about us and directs the sun to cover its blazing lamp. Love comes and says, "Sleep sweetly, my child; I give you sleep." Have you not known what it is at times to lie upon your bed and try in vain to fall asleep? As it is said of Darius, so might it be said of you, that he sent for his musicians, but *his sleep fled from him* (Daniel 6:18). You have attempted to lay hold of sleep, but it escaped you. The more you tried to sleep, the more surely you were awake.

It is beyond our power to acquire a healthy rest. You think that if you fix your mind upon a certain subject until it holds all your attention, you will then sleep, but you find yourself unable to do so. Ten thousand things go through your brain as if the whole earth were whirled before you. You see all kinds of things dancing in wild confusion before your eyes. You close your eyes, but you still see, and there are things in your ears, head, and brain that will not let you find rest. Sleep has forsaken the bed whereon you seek its power.

> Sleep is the best physician that I know of.

It is God alone who gives both the child sleep and the monarch rest, for even with all his power and wealth, the king could not sleep without the aid of God, but would toss to and fro and envy his servant to whom sheer weariness became the friendly administrator of slumber. It is God who drenches the mind in Lethe[9] and provides us with sleep so that our bodies may be refreshed, so that for tomorrow's toil we can rise refreshed and strengthened.

How thankful we should be for sleep! Sleep is the best physician that I know of. Sleep has healed more pains of wearied heads, hearts, and bones than the most eminent physicians upon earth. It is the best medicine. It is the finest thing of all the names that are written in all the lists of the pharmacy. No magic mixture of the physician can match sleep.

What a mercy it is that it belongs alike to all! God does

---

9    Lethe is a mythical river that caused people who drank of its waters to forget what they had done and what they had gone through while they were alive.

not make sleep the aid only of the rich or noble so that they can monopolize it as a peculiar luxury for themselves, but He bestows it upon the poorest and most obscure. If there is any difference, *The sleep of the servant is sweet whether he eats little or much, but the abundance of the rich will not suffer him to sleep* (Ecclesiastes 5:12). He who labors hardest sleeps all the sounder for his work. While luxurious delicacy cannot rest, tossing itself from side to side upon a bed of feathers, the hard-working laborer, with his strong and powerful limbs, worn out and tired, throws himself upon his hard couch and sleeps – and when he wakes up, he thanks God that he has been refreshed.

You do not know how much you owe to God for giving you rest at night. If you had sleepless nights, you would then value the blessing. If for weeks you lay tossing on your weary bed, you then would thank God for this favor. As sleep is the merciful appointment of God, it is a gift most precious, one that cannot be valued until it is taken away – and even then, we cannot appreciate it as we should.

The psalmist says there are some people who are so foolish that they deny themselves sleep. For purposes of gain, or ambition, they rise early and sit up late. *It is vain for you to rise up early, to come home late, to eat the bread of sorrows, because he shall give his beloved sleep* (Psalm 127:2). We may have been guilty of the same thing. We have risen early in the morning that we might read about a new business method. We have sat up at night until we have seen the sun rising. While our eyes have ached, our brain has throbbed and our heart has palpitated. We have been weary and worn out. We have risen early and sat up late, and in that way we have come to eat the bread of sorrow by failing health and depressed spirits.

Many of you businessmen are working in that way. We do not condemn you for it. We do not forbid rising up early and staying up late, but we remind you of this text: *It is vain for you to rise up early, to come home late, to eat the bread of sorrows, because he shall give his beloved sleep.*

Sleep is frequently used in a bad sense in the Word of God in order to express the condition of carnal and worldly men. Some people have the sleep of carnal ease and sloth, of whom Solomon tells us that they are unwise sons who slumber in the harvest, causing shame. *He that gathers in summer is a wise son, but he that sleeps in harvest is a son that causes shame* (Proverbs 10:5). *The harvest is past, the summer is ended, and we are not saved* (Jeremiah 8:20).

Sleep often expresses a state of idleness, deadness, and indifference in which all ungodly people are found, according to the words, *It is high time to awaken ourselves out of sleep* (Romans 13:11), and *Let us not sleep, as do others; but let us watch and be sober* (1 Thessalonians 5:6). There are many who are sleeping the sluggard's sleep, who are tossing upon the bed of idle ease. A terrible waking awaits them, though, when they will find that the time of their proving has been wasted. The golden sands of their lives have dropped unheeded from the hourglass, and they have come into that world where there are no acts of pardon passed, no hope, no refuge, and no salvation.

In other places you find sleep used as the figure of carnal security, in which so many are found. Look at Saul, lying asleep in fleshly security. He is not like David, who said, *I will both lay me down in peace and sleep: for thou only, O LORD, dost make me to be confident* (Psalm 4:8). Abner, the captain of Saul's host, was there, and all the troops lay around him, but Abner slept. Sleep on, Saul! Sleep on! Abishai is standing close by, and with a spear in his hand he says, *Let me smite him, I pray thee, with the spear and pin him to the earth at once* (1 Samuel 26:8). Still he sleeps. He does not know that he is on the brink of the eternal sleep!

This is how many of you are – sleeping in jeopardy of your

souls. Satan is standing over you, the law is ready to smite you, and vengeance is prepared. Even Providence seems to say, "Shall I smite him? I will smite him but this once, and he will never wake again." Jesus intervenes and cries, "Not yet, vengeance, restrain yourself!" Even now the spear is quivering! "Not yet! Spare the sleeper yet one more year in the hope that he may yet awake from this long sleep of sin."

Like Sisera, I tell you, sinner, you are sleeping in the tent of the destroyer (Judges 4). You may have eaten off a kingly dish, but you are sleeping on the doorstep of hell. Even now the Enemy is lifting up the hammer and nail to smite you through your temples and fasten you to the earth so that you may lie forever in that death of everlasting torment that is so much worse than common death.

There is also the sleep of negligence, such as the foolish virgins had, when it is said, *They all slumbered and slept* (Matthew 25:5). There is the sleep of sorrow, which overcame Peter, James, and John in the garden of Gethsemane (Matthew 26). But none of these are the gifts of God. They result from the frailty of our nature. They come upon us because we are fallen people. They creep over us because we are children of a lost and ruined parent. These sleeps are not the gifts of God, nor does He bestow them on His beloved.

# Chapter 12

# An Innkeeper's Prayer

I t is said that Rowland Hill[10] once had to spend the night in a village where there was no other house to stay in but a tavern. Having a pair of horses to feed, and going into the best room of the inn, he was considered to be a valuable guest for the night. So the host came in and said, "Glad to see you, Mr. Hill."

"I am going to stay with you tonight," was the reply. "Will you let me have family prayer tonight in this house?"

"I never had such a thing as family prayer here," said the landlord, "and I don't want to have it now."

"Very well; then just bring me my horses. I can't stay in a house where they won't pray to God. Bring the horses out."

Being too good a guest to lose, the man thought better of it and promised to have family prayer. "Ah," said Hill. "I'm not in the habit of conducting prayer in other people's houses. You must conduct it yourself."

The man said he could not pray. "But you must," said Rowland Hill.

"Oh, but I have never prayed."

"Then, my dear man, you will begin tonight," was the answer.

---

10    Rowland Hill (1744-1833) was an English evangelical preacher.

The time came, and the family members were on their knees.

"Now," said Rowland Hill, "every man prays in his own house. You must offer prayer tonight."

"I can't pray. I can't!" said the landlord.

"What, man? You have had all these mercies today, and are you so ungrateful that you cannot thank God for them? Besides, what a wicked sinner you have been! Can't you tell God what a sinner you've been and ask for pardon?"

The man began to cry, "I can't pray, Mr. Hill. I can't – indeed, I can't."

"Then tell the Lord, man, you can't. Tell Him you can't pray," said Mr. Hill, "and ask Him to help you."

Down went the poor landlord on his knees. "O Lord, I can't pray. I wish I could."

"Ah! You have begun to pray," said Rowland Hill. "You have begun to pray, and you will never stop praying. As soon as God has set you to begin praying, weak though your praying may be, you will never stop praying. Now I'll pray for you."

And so he did, and it was not long before the Lord was pleased, through that strange method, to break the landlord's hard heart and to bring him to Christ. If any of you can't pray, tell the Lord you can't. Ask Him to help you pray. Ask Him to show you your need to be saved – and if you can't pray, ask Him to give you everything that you need. Christ will *make* the message as well as *take* the message. He will put His own blood upon your prayer, and the Father will send the Holy Spirit down to you to give you more faith and more trust in Christ.

# Chapter 13

# Punishment of Evildoers

S ome time ago, an excellent lady wanted to talk with me, with the object, as she said, of gaining my support upon the topic of anti-capital punishment. I heard the excellent reasons she urged against hanging people who had committed murder, and although they did not convince me, I did not seek to reply to them. She suggested that when someone committed murder, he should be imprisoned for life. I told her that many men who had been imprisoned half their lives were not a bit better for it. As for her belief that they would necessarily be brought to repentance, I was afraid it was but a dream.

"Ah!" she said, good soul as she was. "That is because we have been all wrong about punishments. We punish people because we think they deserve to be punished. We ought to show them," she said, "that we love them – that we only punish them to make them better."

"Indeed, madam," I said, "I have heard that theory a great many times, and I have seen much fine writing upon the matter, but I am no believer in it. The design of punishment should be change, but the basis of punishment lies in the positive guilt of the offender. I believe that when a man does wrong, he ought to be punished for it, and that there is a guilt in sin that justly merits punishment."

"Oh, no!" She could not see that. Sin was a very wrong thing, but punishment was not a proper idea. She thought that people were treated too cruelly in prison and that they ought to be taught that we love them. If they were treated kindly in prison, and tenderly dealt with, they would grow so much better, she was sure.

With a view of interpreting her own theory, I said, "I suppose, then, you would give criminals all sorts of indulgences in prison. Some wicked vagabond who has committed burglary dozens of times – I suppose you would let him sit in an easy chair in the evening before a nice fire, mix him a glass of alcohol and water, give him his pipe, and make him happy to show him how much we love him."

"Well, no," she said. "I would not give him the alcohol, but still, all the rest would do him good."

I thought that was certainly a delightful picture. It seemed to me to be the most prolific method of cultivating criminals and dishonest people that ingenuity could invent. I imagine that you could grow any number of thieves in that way. It would be a special means of propagating all manner of crime and wickedness. These very delightful theories, to such a simple mind as mine, were the source of much amusement. The idea of coddling criminals and treating their crimes as if they were the tumbles and falls of children made me laugh heartily. I imagined that I could picture the government turning its functions over to these excellent people, along with the grand results of their marvelously kind experiments. The sword of the magistrate would be transformed into a spoon for food, and the jail would become a sweet retreat for injured reputations.

Little, however, did I think I would live to see these kinds of things taught in pulpits. I had no idea that there would be pastors who would bring down God's moral government from the solemn aspect in which Scripture reveals it, to a spineless sentimentalism that adores a deity destitute of every masculine virtue.

We never know today what will occur tomorrow. We have lived to see a certain sort of person – thank God they are not Baptists, though I am sorry to say there are a great many Baptists who are beginning to follow in their trail – who seek to teach nowadays that God is a universal Father and that our ideas of His dealing with the impenitent as a Judge, and not as a Father, are remnants of old-fashioned error. Sin, according to these people, is a disorder rather than an offense, an error rather than a crime. Love is the only attribute they can discern, and they have not known the complete Deity.

Some of these men push their way very far into the bogs and mire of falsehood – until they inform us that eternal punishment is to be ridiculed as a dream. In fact, books now appear that teach us that there is no such thing as the vicarious sacrifice of our Lord Jesus Christ – that Jesus did not die in our place. They use the word *atonement*, it is true, but regarding its meaning they have removed the ancient landmark. They acknowledge that the Father has shown His great love to poor sinful man by sending His Son, but not that God was inflexibly just in the demonstration of His mercy nor that He punished Christ on behalf of His people. They do not acknowledge that God will ever punish anybody in His wrath or that there is such a thing as justice apart from discipline. Even *sin* and *hell* are but old words to them, used now in a new and altered sense. They call them old-fashioned notions, and they say that we poor souls who go on talking about election and imputed righteousness are behind our time.

> Sin, according to these people, is a disorder rather than an offense, an error rather than a crime.

I have often thought the best answer for all these new ideas is that the true gospel was always preached to the poor: *The poor have the gospel preached to them* (Matthew 11:5). I am sure that the poor or the rich will never learn the gospel of these new ministers, for they cannot make head nor tail of it. After you have read through one of their volumes, you do not have the least idea of what the book is about until you have read it through eight or nine times, and then you begin to think you are a very stupid being for ever having read such elaborate heresy, for it sours your temper and makes you feel angry to see the precious truths of God trodden under foot.

Some of us must stand out against these attacks on truth, although we do not love controversy. We rejoice in the liberty of our fellow men and want them to proclaim their convictions, but if they touch these precious things, they touch the apple of our eye. We can allow a thousand opinions in the world, but that which infringes upon the precious doctrine of a covenant salvation through the imputed righteousness of our Lord Jesus Christ – against that we must, and will, enter our fervent and solemn protest, as long as God spares us. Take away once from us those glorious doctrines, and where are we, brethren? We can lay down and die, for nothing remains that is worth living for. If we find these doctrines to be untrue, we have come to the valley of the shadow of death. If these things are not the truths of Christ, if they are not true, there is no comfort left for any poor man under God's sky, and it would be better for us never to have been born.

I can say what Jonathan Edwards says at the end of one of his books:

"If any man could disprove the doctrines of the
gospel, he should then sit down and weep to
think they were not true, for it would be the most

dreadful calamity that could happen to the world, to have a glimpse of such truths, and then for them to melt away in the thin air of fiction, as having no substantiality in them."

Stand up for the truth of Christ. I do not want you to be bigoted, but I do want you to have unwavering beliefs. Do not support any of this trash and error that is going abroad, but stand firm. Do not be turned away from your steadfastness by any pretense of intellectuality and high philosophy, but *earnestly persevere in the faith which was given once unto the saints* (Jude v. 3), and *hold fast the form of sound words* which you have heard from us (2 Timothy 1:13), and have been taught, even as you have read in the Bible, which is the way of everlasting life.

# Chapter 14

# Priceless Life

Once when Rowland Hill was preaching, Lady Ann Erskine happened to be riding by. She asked the coachman what all the people were there for. He replied, "They are going to hear Rowland Hill."

Well, she had heard a great deal about this strange man, considered to be the very wildest of preachers, and so she drew near. No sooner did Rowland Hill see her, than he said to the crowd, "Come. I am going to have an auction. I am going to sell Lady Ann Erskine." She, of course, stopped, and she wondered how she was going to be disposed of. Rowland Hill played the part of both the auctioneer and the bidder:

"Who will buy her? Here comes the world to bid. What will you give for her?"

"I will give her all the splendor and vanities of this present life; she will be a happy woman here. She will be very rich, she will have many admirers, and she will go through this world with many joys."

"You cannot have her. Her soul is an everlasting thing. It is a poor price you are offering. You are only giving a little. As it says in Mark 8:36, what will it profit her if she gains the whole world and loses her own soul?"

"Here comes another purchaser – here is the devil. What will you give for her?"

"Well," he says, "I will let her enjoy the pleasures of sin for a season. She will indulge in everything her heart will set itself unto. She will have everything to delight the eye and the ear. She will indulge in every sin and vice that can possibly give a temporary pleasure."

"Ah, Satan! What will you do for her forever? You cannot have her, for I know what you are. You would give a meager price for her and then destroy her soul to all eternity."

"But here comes another. I know Him – it is the Lord Jesus. What will you give for her?"

"He says, 'It is not what I will give; it is what I have given. I have given My life. I have given My blood for her. I have bought her with a price, and I will give her heaven forever and ever. I will give her grace in her heart now and glory throughout eternity.'"

"O Lord Jesus Christ, You will have her. Lady Ann Erskine, do you object to the bargain?" She was completely caught off guard. There was no answer that could be given.

"It is done," he said. "It is done. You are the Savior's. I have betrothed you unto Him; never break that contract."

And she never did. From that time forth, from being a light-hearted and inconsistent woman she became one of the most serious persons and one of the greatest supporters of the truth of the gospel in those times. She died in a glorious and certain hope of entering the kingdom of heaven. Whosoever is willing to have Christ, Christ is willing to have him.

# Chapter 15

# No Excuse for Ignorance

Every person in his calling has a sermon preached to him. The farmer has a thousand sermons. He does not need to go an inch without hearing the Lord inviting him to righteousness, for all nature round about him has a tongue given to it, when man has an ear to hear.

There are others, however, engaged in work that does not allow them to see much of nature, yet even there, God has provided them with a lesson. There is the baker who provides us with our bread. He thrusts his fuel into the oven, causes it to glow with heat, and puts bread therein. If he is an ungodly person, he should well tremble as he stands at the oven's mouth, for there is a text that he should consider as he stands there: *The day comes that shall burn as an oven; and all the proud, and all that do wickedly shall be stubble* (Malachi 4:1). They will be consumed. The baker should also consider this: *He who does not abide in me shall be cast forth as an unsound branch and shall wither, and they are gathered and cast into the fire and are burned* (John 15:6). Out of the oven's mouth comes a hot and burning warning, and the baker's heart might melt like wax within him if he would only consider it.

Then see the butcher. How does the beast speak to him? He sees the lamb almost lick his knife, and the bullock goes unconsciously to the slaughter. How might he think every time that he strikes the unconscious animal – who knows nothing of death – of his own doom! Are we not, all of us who are without Christ, being made ready for the slaughter? Are we not more foolish than the bullock, for does not the wicked man follow his executioner and walk after his own destroyer into the very chambers of hell? When we see a drunkard pursuing his drunkenness, or an unprincipled man running in the way of immorality, is he not as an ox going to the slaughter, until a dart smites him through the liver (Proverbs 7:22-23)? Has not God sharpened His knife and made ready His ax so that the fatlings of this earth can be killed and the birds of the air and the beasts of the field will feast on the slain (Ezekiel 39:4; Jeremiah 7:33)? Yes, butcher, there is a lecture for you in your trade, and your business may reproach you.

To you whose craft is to sit still all day, making shoes for our feet – the lapstone in your lap may reproach you, for your heart, perhaps, is as hard as that. Have you not been smitten as often as your lapstone, and yet your heart has never been broken or melted? What will the Lord say to you at last, when your stony heart is still within you? He will condemn you and cast you away because you would not heed any of His rebukes, and you would not turn at the voice of His exhortation.

Let the brewer remember that as he brews, so he must drink. Let the potter tremble that he does not end up like a vessel marred upon the wheel. Let the printer take heed that his life is set in heavenly type and not in the black letter of sin. Painter, beware, for paint will not suffice; we must have unvarnished realities!

You who work in a business where you are continually weighing or measuring things – you can weigh and measure yourself daily by the standard of the Word of God. You can imagine that you saw the great Judge standing by with His gospel in one scale and you in the other, and solemnly looking down upon you, saying, *MENE, MENE, TEKEL, UPHARSIN. TEKEL; Thou art weighed in the balances and art found wanting* (Daniel 5:25, 27).

Some of you might measure out lengths or portions for your customers. Think of your life too. It is to be of a certain length, and every year moves the tape measure a little farther, and at last, the scissors will clip off your life, and it is over. How do you know when you have come to the last inch? What is that disease that you have, but the first snip of the scissors? What is that trembling in your bones, that failing of your eyesight, that fleeing of your memory, that departure of your youthful vigor, but the first rip of the fabric? How soon you will be torn in two, the remnant of your days passed away, and your years all numbered and gone, misspent and wasted forever!

**As is your labor, so will your end be.**

Maybe you work as a general laborer, and your duties are diverse. Then diverse are the lectures God preaches to you. *Man certainly has an appointed amount of time upon earth, and his days are like the days of a hireling. As a slave earnestly desires the shade and as a hireling waits for rest from his work, so I am made to possess months of vanity, and wearisome nights are appointed to me* (Job 7:1-3). There is a similarity for you, when you have fulfilled your time on earth and will receive your wages at last. Who, then, is your master? Are you serving Satan and the lusts of the flesh, and will you receive your wages in the hot metal of destruction? Or are you serving the fair Prince Emmanuel, and your wages will be the golden crowns of heaven? Oh, happy you are if you serve a good Master! According to your master will be your reward. As is your labor, so will your end be.

Are you a person who writes for a living? Know that your life is a writing. When your hand is not on the pen, you are a writer still, for you are always writing upon the pages of eternity. You are always writing either your sins or your holy confidence in Him who loved you. Happy it will be for you, O writer, if your name is written in the Lamb's Book of Life, and if that black writing of yours, in the history of your pilgrimage below, will have been blotted out with the red blood of Christ, for then you will have the mighty name of the Lord written upon you, to stand legible forever.

Maybe you are a physician or a pharmacist and you prescribe or prepare medicines for the body. God stands there by the side of your medicines and by the table where you write your prescriptions, and He says to you, "You are yourself sick. I can prescribe the cure for you. The blood and righteousness of Christ, laid hold of by faith and applied by the Spirit, can cure your soul. I can make a medicine for you that will get rid of all that troubles you and will bring you to the place where the inhabitants will no more say, 'I am sick.' Will you take my medicine or will you reject it? Is it bitter to you, and do you refuse it? Come and drink, my child; drink, for your life lies here, and *how will we escape if we neglect so great a salvation*" (Hebrews 2:3 NASB)?

Do you cast iron, melt lead, or fuse the hard metals of the mines? Then pray that the Lord will melt your heart and cast you in the mold of the gospel.

Do you make clothing? Be careful that you find a garment for yourself forever. *I will rejoice greatly in the Lord, I will rejoice greatly in the Lord, My soul will exult in my God; For He has clothed me with garments of salvation, He has wrapped me with a robe of righteousness, As a bridegroom decks himself with a garland, And as a bride adorns herself with her jewels.* (Isaiah 61:10 NASB).

Are you busy building all day long, laying one stone upon

another and setting the mortar in its crevice? Then remember that you are building for eternity too. Oh, that you might yourself be built upon a good foundation! Oh, that you might build thereon, not wood, hay, or stubble, but gold, silver, and precious stones, and things that will abide the fire! *Now if anyone builds upon this foundation gold, silver, precious stones, wood, hay, stubble, the work of each one shall be made manifest, for the day shall declare it because it shall be revealed by fire; the work of each one, whatever sort it is, the fire shall put it to test* (1 Corinthians 3:12-13).

**Remember that you are building for eternity too.**

Take care that you are truly God's scaffold, so that you are not used on earth to be a scaffolding for building His church, and when His church is built you will be cast down and burned up with fire unquenchable (Matthew 3:12). Take care that you are built upon a rock and not upon the sand (Matthew 7:24-27), and that the red cement of the Savior's precious blood unites you to the foundation of the building and to every stone thereof.

Are you a jeweler, and do you cut your gems and polish diamonds every day? Then take warning from the contrast that your life is to the stone on which you exercise your craft! You cut it, and it glitters more, the more you cut it; but even though you have been cut and ground, even though you have been sick and have been at death's door many times, you do not shine any brighter, but appear even duller, for sadly, you are no diamond. You are only a pebble from the brook, and in that day when God makes up His jewels, He will not include you in His chest of treasures, for you are not one of the precious sons of Zion, comparable unto fine gold. *The sons of Zion, precious and esteemed more than pure gold, how are they taken for earthen vessels, the work of the hands of the potter!* (Lamentations 4:2).

Whatever your situation is, whatever your occupation, there

is a continual sermon preached to your conscience. I wish that from now on you would open your eyes and ears and see and hear the things that God desires to teach you.

# Chapter 16

# We Must Pray

Poor Ananias was afraid to go to Saul. He thought it was very much like stepping into a lion's den. "If I go to his house," he thought, "the moment he sees me, he will take me to Jerusalem at once, for I am one of Christ's disciples. I dare not go."

God says, "Behold, he prays."

"Well," says Ananias, "that is enough for me. If he is a praying man, he will not hurt me. If he is a man of real devotion, I am safe" (Acts 9:1-17).

You can be sure that you can always trust a praying person. I do not know how it is, but even most ungodly people seem to pay reverence to a sincere Christian. An employer likes to have a praying employee. If the employer does not care about being a Christian himself, he likes to have a pious employee, and he will trust him more than any other. True, there are some professedly praying people who do not have a bit of prayer in them, but whenever you find a real praying person, you can trust him with untold gold. If he really prays, you do not need to be afraid of him. He who communes with God in secret can be trusted in public. I always feel safe with a man who is a visitor to the mercy seat.

I heard an anecdote about two gentlemen who were traveling together somewhere in Switzerland. They soon came into the midst of the forests, and you know the gloomy tales the people were accustomed to tell about the inns in the lone places and how dangerous it is to lodge in them. Well, one of the travelers, an infidel, said to the other man, who was a Christian, "I don't like stopping here at all. It is a very eerie-looking house."

"Well," said the other, "let us try." So they went into the house, but it looked so mysterious that neither of them liked it. There was no doubt that they would have greatly preferred being at home in England.

Soon, however, the landlord said, "Gentlemen, I always read and pray with my family before going to bed; will you allow me to do so tonight?"

"Yes," they said, "with the greatest pleasure."

When they went upstairs, the infidel said, "I am not at all afraid now."

"Why not?" asked the Christian.

"Because our host has prayed."

"Oh!" said the other. "Then it seems, after all, that you do think something about Christianity. Because a man prays, you can go to sleep in his house without fear of being robbed or murdered."

It was marvelous how both slept. They had sweet dreams, for they felt that where the house had been roofed by prayer and walled with devotion, no one would do them wrong. This, then, was an argument to Ananias, that he might go with safety to Saul's lodging.

Mrs. Berry used to say, "I would not leave my prayer closet for a thousand worlds." Mr. Jay said, "If the twelve apostles were living near you and you had access to them, if this fellowship drew you from prayer, they would prove a real injury to your souls." Prayer is the ship that brings home the richest freight from the celestial shores. Prayer is the soil that yields the most abundant harvest.

Brother, when you rise in the morning, your business so urgent, that with a hurried word or two of prayer, out you go into the world; and at night, worn out and tired, you give God the meager leftovers of the day – the consequence is that you have no communion with Him. The reason we do not have more true Christianity among us now is because we do not have more secret prayer.

> The reason we do not have more true Christianity among us now is because we do not have more secret prayer.

I have something to say about the churches of the present day that do not spend much time in real prayer. Say to your minister, "Sir, we must have more prayer." Urge the people to more prayer. Have a prayer meeting, even if you have it all to yourself; and if you are asked how many were present, you can say, "Four."

"Four! How so?"

"Well, I was there, and so were God the Father, God the Son, and God the Holy Spirit – and we had deep and real communion together."

We must have an outpouring of real devotion, or else what is to become of many of our churches? Oh, may God awaken us all and stir us up to pray, for when we pray, we will be victorious! I would like to take you, as Samson did the foxes (Judges 15:4-5), tie the firebrands of prayer to you, and send you in among the shocks of corn until you set the whole field ablaze. I would like to make a blaze by my words and set all the churches on fire with zeal for God's glory.

# Chapter 17

# Popular Errors

There are many people who think that salvation cannot be accomplished except in some undefinable and mysterious way – and the minister and the preacher are mixed up with it. Hear me, then: if you had never seen a minister in your life, if you had never heard the voice of the minister or the pastor of the church, yet if you did call upon the name of the Lord, your salvation would be just as certain without one as with one.

We are all clergy if we love the Lord Jesus Christ, and you are as much fit to preach the gospel if God has given you the ability and called you to the work by His Spirit, as any man alive. No priestly hand, no group of elders, no ordination of men is necessary. We stand upon the rights of manhood to speak what we believe, and next to that we stand upon the call of God's Spirit in the heart bidding us to testify to His truth.

Neither Paul nor an angel from heaven, nor Apollos, nor Cephas, can help you in salvation. It is not of man, neither by men, and no pope, archbishop, bishop, priest, minister, or anyone has any grace to give to others. We must each go ourselves to the fountainhead, pleading this promise: *For whosoever shall call upon the name of the Lord shall be saved* (Romans 10:13).

If I were shut up in the mines of Siberia, where I could never hear the gospel, if I would call upon the name of Christ, the road is just as straight without the minister as with him, and the path to heaven is just as clear from the wilds of Africa and from the dens of the prison house and the dungeon as it is from the sanctuary of God. Nevertheless, for edification, all Christians love the ministry, though not for salvation. True Christians do not put their trust in priest or preacher, yet the Word of God is sweet to them. *How lovely on the mountains Are the feet of him who brings good news, Who announces peace And brings good news of happiness, Who announces salvation, And says to Zion, "Your God reigns!* (Isaiah 52:7 NASB).

Another very common error is that a good dream is a most splendid thing in order to save people. Some of you do not know the extent to which this error prevails. I happen to know it. Many people believe that if you dream that you see the Lord in the night, you will be saved, and if you can see Him on the cross, if you think you see some angels, or if you dream that God says to you, "You are forgiven," all is well.

That is simply rubbish! There is nothing of truth in it. Dreams – the disordered fabrics of a wild imagination, the unsteadiness, often of the fair pillars of a grand conception, how can they be the means of salvation?

I must quote Rowland Hill in default of a better answer. When a woman pleaded that she was saved because she dreamed, he said, "Well, my good woman, it is very nice to have good dreams when you are asleep, but I want to see how you act when you are awake; for if your conduct is not consistent in your Christianity when you are awake, I will not give a snap of the finger for your dreams."

I marvel that any person would ever go to such a depth of ignorance as to tell me the stories that I have heard about dreams. Poor dear creatures! When they were sound asleep, they saw the gates of heaven opened, a white angel came and washed their sins away, and then they saw that they were pardoned – and since then they have never had a doubt or a fear. It is time – a very good time – that you should begin to doubt, then, for if that is all the hope you have, it is a poor one.

Remember, it is *whosoever shall call upon the name of the Lord*, not whosoever dreams about Him. Dreams may do good. Sometimes people have been frightened out of their senses in them, and they were better out of their senses than they were in them, for they did more mischief when they were in their senses than they did when they were out – and the dreams did good in that sense. Some people, too, have been alarmed by dreams; but to trust in them is to trust in a shadow, to build your hopes on bubbles, scarcely needing a puff of wind to burst them into nothingness. Oh, remember, you do not need a vision or some supernatural appearance! If you have had a vision or a dream, you do not need to despise it. It may have benefited you, but do not trust in it. If you have not had such a dream, remember that God's promise of salvation comes by you calling upon His name, not by having a dream.

There are some people who think they must have some very wonderful kind of emotion or feelings in order to be saved. Some think that they must have some most extraordinary thoughts such as they never had before, or else they cannot be saved.

A woman once came to me and wanted to become a member of the church. I asked her whether she had ever had a change of heart. She said, "Oh yes, sir, such a change! You know," she said, "I felt it across the chest so remarkably, sir, and when I was praying one day, I felt as if I did not know what was the matter with me, I felt so different. And when I went to the chapel, sir, one night, I came away and felt so different from what I felt before; I felt so light."

"Yes," I said, "light-headed, my dear soul. That is what you felt, but nothing more, I am afraid."

The good woman was sincere enough. She thought everything was all right with her because something had affected her lungs or had in some way stirred her physical frame. "No," I hear you say, "people cannot be so foolish as this." I assure you that there are many who have no better hope of heaven than that, for I am dealing with a very popular objection just now.

"I thought," one person said, addressing me one day, "when I was in the garden, that Christ could surely take my sins away just as easily as He could move the clouds. Do you know, sir, that in a moment or two the cloud was gone and the sun was shining? I thought to myself, *The Lord is blotting out my sin.*"

Such a ridiculous thought as that, you say, could not occur often, but I tell you it does – very frequently indeed. Some people think that the greatest nonsense in all the earth is a manifestation of divine grace in their hearts.

The only feeling I ever want to have is this: I want to feel that I am a sinner and that Christ is my Savior. You can keep your visions, feelings, and excited emotionalism to yourselves. The only feeling that I desire to have is deep repentance and humble faith in Christ; and if, poor sinner, you have that, you are saved.

Some people believe that before they can be saved there must be a kind of electric shock, some very wonderful thing that is to go all through them from head to foot. Now hear this: *The word is near thee, even in thy mouth and in thy heart: that is, the word of faith, which we preach, that if thou shalt confess with thy mouth the Lord Jesus and shalt believe in thine heart that God has raised him from the dead, thou shalt be saved* (Romans 10:8-9). What do you want with all this nonsense of dreams and supernatural thoughts? All that is needed is that as a guilty sinner, I should come and cast myself on Christ. Having done that, the soul is safe, and all the visions in the universe could not make it safer.

I now have one more error to try to rectify. Among very poor people – and I have visited some of them and I know that what I say is true – among the very poor and uneducated, there is a very current idea that somehow or other salvation is connected with learning to read and write. You smile, perhaps, but I know it. Often has a poor woman said, "Oh sir, this is no good to poor, ignorant creatures like us. There is no hope for me, sir. I cannot read. Do you know, sir, I don't know a single letter? I think if I could read a bit, I might be saved, but as ignorant as I am, I do not know how I can be, for I have got no understanding, sir."

I have found this in the country districts too, among people who could learn to read if they wanted to. And there are none who cannot, unless they are lazy. Yet they sit down in cold indifference about salvation, under the notion that the preacher could be saved, for he reads a chapter so nicely; the clerk could be saved, for he said "Amen" so well; the rich gentleman could be saved, for he knew a great deal and had many books in his library – but that they could not be saved, for they did not know anything, and therefore it was impossible. My poor friend, you do not need to know much to go to heaven. I would advise you to learn as much as you can; do not be backward in trying to learn. But in regard to going to heaven, the way is so plain, that *the foolish shall not err therein* (Isaiah 35:8).

# Chapter 18

# Don't Wait Until You're Dying

I t is astonishing for how little price a person will sell his soul. I remember an anecdote that I believe is true. A minister, going across some fields, met a country dweller and said to him, "Well, friend, it is a most delightful day."

"Yes, sir, it is."

The minister spoke to him about the beauties of the scenery and so forth, and then he said, "How thankful we ought to be for our mercies! I hope you never come out without praying."

"Pray, sir!" he said. "Why, I never pray; I have got nothing to pray for."

"What a strange man you are!" said the minister. "Doesn't your wife pray?"

"If she wants to."

"Don't your children pray?"

"If they want to, they do."

The minister, realizing that the man was irrational, said, "Well, then, you mean to say you do not pray. I will give you five dollars if you will promise me not to pray as long as you live."

"Very well," said the man. "I don't see what I have got to pray for," and he took the five dollars. When he went home, the thought struck him, *What have I done?* Something said to him, *Well, John, you will die soon, and you will want to pray then. You will have to stand before your Judge, and it will be a sad thing never to have prayed.*

Thoughts of this kind came over him, and he felt dreadfully miserable. The more he thought, the more miserable he felt. His wife asked him what was the matter. He could hardly tell her for some time, but at last he confessed that he had taken five dollars never to pray again, and that was troubling his mind. The poor ignorant soul thought it was the Evil One who had appeared to him in that field.

"Yes, John," said his wife. "Sure enough, it was the devil, and you have sold your soul to him for that five dollars." The poor man could not work for several days, and he became completely miserable from the conviction that he had sold himself to the Evil One. However, the minister knew what was happening, and there was a barn close by. He was going to preach there, and he guessed that the man would be there to ease his terror of mind.

Sure enough, he was there one Sunday evening, and he heard the same man who gave him the five dollars take Mark 8:36 for his text: *For what shall it profit a man, if he shall gain the whole world and lose his own soul?* "Yes," said the preacher, "what will it profit a man who sold his soul for five dollars?"

The man stood up and cried out, "Sir, take it back! Take it back!"

"Why?" said the minister. "You wanted the five dollars, and you said you did not need to pray."

"But sir," he said, "I must pray. If I do not pray, I am lost." After some negotiation and discussion, the five dollars was returned, and the man was on his knees praying to God. That very circumstance was the means of saving his soul and making him a changed man.

# Chapter 19

# Our Days Are Numbered

A present God! I cannot suggest a theme that can make you more full of courage in times of danger and trouble. You will find it exceedingly helpful and comforting if you can discover God in the little things. Our life is made up of little things, and if we had a God only for the big things and not for the little things, we would be miserable indeed. If we had a God of the temple and not a God of the tents of Jacob, where would we be? But, blessed be our heavenly Father, it is He who wings an angel and guides a sparrow. It is God who rolls the world along and also molds a tear and marks its orbit when it trickles from its source. God is as much the initiator of the motion of a grain of dust blown by the summer wind as He is of the revolutions of the stupendous planet. God is as in control of the sparkling of a firefly as much as the fiery comet.

I implore you to carry home to your houses the thought that God is there with you at your table, in your bedroom, in your workroom, and at your kitchen table. Recognize the doing and God in every little thing. Think for a moment, and you will find that there are many promises of Scripture that prove the sweetest consolation in trivial matters. *For he shall give his angels charge over thee to keep thee in all thy ways. They shall bear thee up in their hands.* Why? So you do not fall from a precipice? So you do not throw yourself from a pinnacle? No: *lest thy foot stumble against a stone* (Psalm 91:11-12). It is only a little danger, but there is a great Providence to keep us from it.

What else does the Bible say? Does it say, "The very days of your life are numbered"? It does not say that, even though that is true, but it says, *the very hairs of your head are all numbered* (Matthew 10:30). What more does the Word of God say? Does it say, "The Lord knows the eagles, and not an eagle falls to the ground without your Father"? No, but it says, *Are not two sparrows sold for a farthing? And one of them shall not fall on the ground without your Father* (Matthew 10:29). He is a great God in little things.

I am sure it will spare you a world of irritation if you will just remember this, for it is from this that our irritations come. We often get into a bad temper about a little thing, when a great trial does not agitate us. We are angry because we have scalded ourselves with a little water or have lost a button from our clothes, and yet the greatest calamity can hardly disturb us. You smile because it is true. Job himself, who said, *The LORD gave, and the LORD has taken away* (Job 1:21), might have gotten angry because of some rough edge in his potsherd. Take care that you see God in little things so that your mind may be always calm and composed, and that you are not foolish enough to allow a little thing to overcome a saint of God.

Our life is entirely dependent upon God. One sees strange sights in traveling – scenes that will never be erased from the memory. It was some years ago, just under an enormous rock, that I saw a huge pile of broken stones and dirt that had been tossed about in wild confusion and raised in huge mounds. My driver said to me, "That is the grave of a village."

Some years ago, there lived upon that spot a joyful and

happy people. They went forth to their daily work and they ate and drank just as people do to this day. One time they saw a gigantic crack in the mountain that hung overhead. They heard alarming noises, but they had heard such sounds before, and the old men said that there might be something coming, but they did not know. All of a sudden, however, without further notice, the whole side of the hill was in motion, and before the villagers could escape from their huts, the village was buried beneath the fallen rocks. There it lies still, and neither bone of man nor piece of the habitation of man has ever been discovered in the wreck. So thoroughly was everything crushed and buried, that nothing, by the most diligent search, was ever discovered.

> You are sitting today as near to the jaws of death as those villagers who are dwelling underneath the rock.

There are many villages standing in a similar position at this day. I passed another spot where there was a shelving mountain, with its layers slanting toward the valley. A town that had been built at the foot had been entirely covered, and a lake had been filled up by one tremendous slide from the top of the hill. Yet there stand new houses still, and people risk living among the graves of their fathers. We are apt to say, "How these people ought to look up every morning and say, 'O Lord, spare this village!' Standing there, where they might be crushed in a moment, where the slightest motion of the earth within would bring down the hill upon them, they ought to lift up their hearts to the Preserving One and say, "Oh, keeper of Israel, keep us both day and night."

However, you and I are in the same position. Though no overhanging crags hover above our homesteads, though no mountain threatens to leap upon our city, yet there are a thousand gates to death. There are other ways besides these that can hurry mortals to their tombs. You are sitting today as near to the jaws of death as those villagers who are dwelling underneath the rock. Oh, that you realized it! One breath choked up, and you are dead. Perhaps your life is a thousand times in danger every moment. As many times as your heart beats, as many times as you take a breath, so many times does your life hang in such jeopardy that it only needs God to will it, and you will fall dead in your seat and will be carried out a pale, lifeless corpse.

There are parts of the mountain passes of the Alps that are such a danger to the traveler that when you traverse them in winter, the muleteers muffle the bells of their beasts so that the mildest sound does not bring down an avalanche of snow and sweep them into the bottomless precipice beneath. You would think that in that situation, the traveler must feel that he is in God's hand. But you are in the same position now, though you do not see it. Simply open the eyes of your spirit, and you may see the avalanche hanging over you today, and the rock trembling toward you at this very moment. Simply let your soul behold the hidden lightnings that God conceals within His hand, and you may soon see that for God to take away your life now, or whenever He pleases, is easier for Him than for you to crush a gnat with your finger.

As it is with our life, so is it with the comforts of life. What would life be without its comforts? Even more, what would it be without its necessities? Yet how absolutely dependent are we upon God for the bread that is the staff of life! I never felt more truly the dependence of man upon his God than I did at the foot of the Alpine pass of the Splugen. I saw in the distance that the whole road was black, as if it had been spread over with heaps of black earth. As we neared it, we discovered it was a mass of locusts in full march – tens of thousands of myriads of them. As we drew nearer, they divided as regularly as if they had been an army, making room for the carriage. No sooner did the carriage pass than the ranks were filled up again, and they went on in their devouring march.

On we went for several miles, and there was nothing to be seen except these creatures, literally covering the ground here and there in thick layers, like a shower of black snow. Then I realized the language of the prophet: *the earth is as the garden of Eden before him, and behind him a desolate wilderness* (Joel 2:3). The locusts had eaten up every green blade. There stood the Indian corn, with just the dry stems, but every green particle was gone. In the front of their march you saw the vines beginning to ripen and the fields of grain hastening to perfection. There stood the poor cottager at his door. The wheat that he had planted and the vines that he had tended would all be eaten and devoured before his own eyes. The pastures were alive with these fiery creatures. When they first entered the field, there was green pasture for the cows of the poor cottagers, but after the locusts were there for an hour, you could take up the dust by handfuls, with nothing else left.

"Ah!" said my guide. "It is a sad thing for these poor people. In a month, those creatures will be as big and as long as my finger, and then they will eat up the trees, including the mulberry trees with which the poor men feed their silkworms and that furnish them with a little wealth. They will devour every green thing until there is nothing left but the bare, dry stems."

They were in armies as countless as the sands of the sea and fierce to look upon, well described by the prophet Joel in his dreadful picture of them as a great army of the Lord. *Ah!* I thought within myself. *If God can sweep this valley and make a waste of it with these little creatures, what a mercy it is that He is a kind and gracious God, or else He might let loose a similar fate on all the people of the earth, and then nothing would stare us in the face but famine, despair, and death!*

We are not simply dependent upon God for the comforts, but for the power to enjoy the comforts. It is an evil that we have seen under the sun, that a man had wealth, riches, and abundance, but did not have power to eat thereof. I have seen people hungry and full of appetite without any bread to eat. But I have seen a sight perhaps more sad – a man with the most luxurious kinds of food, to whom taste seemed denied, to whom every mouthful was a thing of detestation.

The Lord only has to decide to smite any of us with only nervousness – that nervousness at which the strong may laugh, but that makes the weak tremble, and everything will become dark before you. He has only to affect some portion of your body, and you will see no brightness in the sun. The very fields will lose their bright color before you. The most happy event will only be a source of deeper gloom. You will look on everything as through a dark glass and see nothing but darkness and despair.

God only has to touch you with sickness, and motion may be misery, and even to lie upon a bed may be a repetition of tortures as you toss from side to side. Worse still, the Lord has only to put His finger on your brain, and you become a raving lunatic, or what may seem better, but more despicable, a driveling idiot. Oh, how little, then, has He to do to overturn your all, to pull down that mighty castle of your joys and darken the windows of your hope! You are, again, for life, for necessities, and for comforts as absolutely in the hand of God as the clay is in the hand of the potter. Your rebellion is but the writhing of a worm. You may murmur, but your murmuring cannot affect Him. You may ask your comrades to join with you against the almighty God, but His purpose will stand fast, and you must submit.

# Chapter 20

# How the World Gives

In the first place, the world gives inadequately and grudgingly. Even the world's best friends have had cause to complain of its disgraceful treatment. In reading the biographies of mighty men whom the world honors, you will soon be convinced that the world is a most ungrateful friend. If you would devote your whole life to serve the world and make it happy, do not think that the world would ever return you so much as a penny.

Robert Burns (1759-1796) is an instance of the world's fine gratitude. He was the world's poet. He wrote of the roaring tankard's foaming. He sang the loves of women and the joys of lust. The world admires him, but what did the world do for him? His whole life was spent in near poverty.

When the time came for Robert Burns to be honored (which was all too late for a buried man), how did they honor him? He had poor relatives. Look to the donation list and see how magnificent the donations they received! They honored him with drinks of whisky, which they drank themselves; that was all they would give him. The devotion of the Scotch drunkards to their poet is a devotion to their drunkenness, not to him.

There are undoubtedly many truehearted people who lament

the sinner as much as they admire the genius, but most people like him no less for his faults. However, if it had been ordained and decreed that every drunkard who honored Burns had to go without his whisky for a week, there would not have been a dozen who would have done it – not even half a dozen. Their honor to him was an honor to themselves. It was an opportunity for drunkenness, at least in thousands of instances.

As I stood by his monument some time ago, I saw around it a most dismal, dingy set of withered flowers, and I thought, *Ah, this is his honor! O Burns! How you have spent your life to have a withered wreath for the world's payment of a life of mighty genius and a flood of marvelous song!* Yes, when the world pays best, she pays nothing, and when she pays least, she pays her flatterers with scorn. She rewards their services with neglect and poverty.

I could quote many statesmen who have spent their entire lives in the world's service, and to whom the world at first cheered on, and they were celebrated everywhere. As they were serving, though, they might have made a little mistake (which might prove not even to have been a mistake when the history books are read with a clearer eye) or they might have done something that was not popular, and the world turns on them. "Down with him!" says the world. "We will have nothing more to do with him." All he may have done before meant nothing to them. One mistake, one flaw in his political career, and "Down with him! Cast him to the dogs! We want nothing to do with him again!"

Ah, the world pays meagerly indeed! What will it do for those it loves the best? When it has done all it can, the last resource of the world is to give a person a title (and what good is that?). They might even give him a little monument and set him up there to bear all types of weather, to be pitilessly exposed to every storm; and there he stands for fools to gaze at, one of the world's great ones paid in stone. It is true that the world has paid that out of its own heart, for that is what the world's heart is made of.

The world pays poorly, but did you ever hear a Christian who complained like that of his Master? "No," he will say. "When I serve Christ, I feel that my work is my wages. Labor for Christ is its own reward. He gives me joy on earth, with a fulness of joy hereafter." *In thy presence is fullness of joy; in thy right hand there are pleasures for evermore* (Psalm 16:11).

Oh, Christ is a good paymaster! *For the wages of sin is death, but the grace of God is eternal life* (Romans 6:23). He who serves Christ may get only a little gold and silver that this world calls precious, but he gets a gold and silver that will never be melted in the last refining fire, that will glitter among the precious things of immortality throughout eternity. The world pays miserably and scantily, but not so with Christ.

> If you serve the world, it will pay you halfheartedly.

If you will serve the world, and you want to have gifts from it, the world will pay you halfheartedly. By *the world*, I mean the religious world just as much as any other part of it. I mean the whole world – religious, political, good, bad, and indifferent – the whole lot of them. If you serve the world, it will pay you halfheartedly.

Let a man spend himself for his fellow creatures' interests, and what will he get for it? Some will praise him, and some will revile him. The people who escape without being reviled in this world are the ones who do nothing at all. He who is most valiant and useful must expect to be most condemned and despised. Those people who are carried upon the waves of popular applause are not the people whose worth is true. Those who really do good must swim against the stream.

The whole list of the world's benefactors is an army of

martyrs. The path of the good is marked all along with blood and fire. The world does not pay the people who really serve it, except with ingratitude. And even when the world does pay, it pays halfheartedly. Did you ever know anyone yet concerning whom the world's mind was completely in agreement? I have never heard of any. Someone might say, "So-and-so is one of the best men of his times!" Go down the next street, and you will hear it said, "He is the biggest scoundrel living." You might hear one person say, "I never heard a man as brilliant as he is." "Oh," says another, "he merely speaks nonsense!" "This newspaper," someone says, "so ably defends the rights of the people!" "Oh," says another, "it seeks to pull down everything that is constitutional and proper!"

The world has never made up its mind about any person yet. There is not a soul living concerning whom the world is unanimous. But when Christ gives anything, He always gives with all His heart. He does not say to His people, "There, I give you this, but still I have half a mind to keep it back." No, Christ gives His heart to all His people.

There is no double-mindedness in Jesus. If we are enabled by free grace to serve Him and to love Him, we can rest quite sure that in the rich reward that His grace will give us, His whole heart will go with every blessing. When Christ blesses the poor needy soul, He does not give with one hand and strike with the other. Rather, He gives him mercies with both His hands – both full – and He asks the sinner simply to receive all that He is willing to give.

Whenever the world gives anything, it gives mostly to those who do not need it. I remember once, when I was a boy, having a dog, which I very much treasured. Some man in the street asked me to give him the dog. I thought that was pretty inconsiderate, and I said as much. A gentleman, however, to whom I told it, said, "Now suppose the Duke of So-and-so"

– who was a great man in the neighborhood – "asked you for the dog. Would you give it to him?"

I said, "I think I would."

He said, "Then you are just like all the world; you would give to those who do not need." Who would object to give anything to the queen? Not a one of us, and yet, perhaps, there is no person in the world who so little needs our gifts. We can always give to those who do not require anything, for we feel that there is some little honor granted to us – an honor bestowed by the reception of the gift.

Now look at Jesus. When He gives to His friends, He gets no honor from them. The honor is in His own free heart that leads Him to give to such poor needy worms. Great people have gone to Christ with mere professions, and they have asked Him to be good to them; but then, at the same time, they have declared that they had a righteousness of their own and did not need much from Him. He has, then, sent them about their business and has given them nothing. He said, *I came not to call the righteous, but sinners to repentance* (Luke 5:32).

Whenever poor lost sinners have gone to Christ, He has never turned one of them away – never. He has given all they could possibly want, and infinitely more than they thought they could ever expect. Might not Jesus say to us, when we ask Him for the blessings of His grace, "You are presumptuous in daring to ask"? Instead of that, He loves to be asked, and He freely and richly gives – *not as the world gives* (John 14:27), for He gives to those who need it most.

There is another view of the world's gifts. The world gives to its friends. Anyone will help his own friends. If we do not help our own relatives and friends, then we are worse than heathens and publicans. *If any provide not for his own and specially for those of his own house, he has denied the faith and is worse than an unbeliever* (1 Timothy 5:8).

But the world generally confines its good wishes and blessings to its own class, friends, and family. It cannot think of giving blessings to its enemies. Did you ever hear yet of the world blessing an enemy? Never. It gives its gifts to its friends, and very meagerly even to them. But Christ gives His gifts even to His enemies. *Not as the world gives*, He may truly say.

The world says, "I must see whether you deserve it. I must see that your case is a good one." The world inquires, and inquires, and inquires again, but Christ only sees that our case is a bad one, and then He gives. He does not want a good case, but a bad case. He knows our necessity, and once discovering our necessity, not even all our sin can stop the hand of His bounty.

Oh, if Jesus would call to mind some of the harsh things we have uttered about Him, He would certainly never bless us – if it were not that His ways are far above our ways. *For as the heavens are higher than the earth, so are my ways higher than your ways, and my thoughts than your thoughts* (Isaiah 55:9). Remember, it was not long ago that you cursed Him, since you laughed at His followers, hated His servants, and could spit upon His Bible. Jesus has cast all that behind His back and loved you anyway. Would the world have done that? Let someone get up and severely criticize others – will they forgive? After forgiving, will they begin to bless? Will they die for their enemies? Oh no! Such a thing never entered into the heart of mankind. But Christ blesses rebels, traitors, and enemies to His cross. He brings them to know His love and to taste of His eternal mercies.

The world always gives in a stingy and selfish manner. Most of us are driven to meagerness. If we give anything away to a poor person, we generally hope that he will not come back again. If we give him a few dollars, it is very often, as we say, to get rid of him. If we show a little charity, it is in the hope that we will not see his face at our door again, for we really do not like the same people continually begging at our door when the world is so full of beggars.

Did you ever hear of anyone who gave a beggar something to encourage him to keep on begging from him? I must confess that I never did such a thing, and I am not likely to begin doing so. But that is just what Christ does. When He gives us a little grace, His motive is to make us ask for more; and when He gives us more grace, it is given with the very motive to make us come and ask again. He gives us silver blessings to inspire us to ask for golden mercies. When we have golden favors, those same mercies are given on purpose to lead us to pray more earnestly and to open our mouth wider so that we may receive more. *I am the LORD thy God, who brought thee out of the land of Egypt; open thy mouth wide, and I will fill it* (Psalm 81:10).

What a strange giver Christ is! What a strange friend, that He gives on purpose to make us ask for more! The more you ask of Christ, the more you *can* ask. The more you have, the more you will want. The more you know Him, the more you will desire to know Him. The more grace you receive, the more grace you will desire. When you are full of grace, you will never be content until you are full of glory. Christ's way of giving is *of his fullness have all we received, and grace for grace* (John 1:16). He gives grace to make us desire more grace; grace to make us yearn after something higher, something fuller and richer still. *Not as the world gives, give I unto you* (John 14:27).

# Chapter 21

# Have Courage

How man has struggled against man! Man is the wolf of mankind. Not even the elements in all their fury nor the wild beasts of prey in all their cruelty have ever been such terrible enemies to man as man has been to his own fellow. When you read the story of the persecution by Queen Mary in England, you are astounded that creatures wearing a human form could ever be so bloodthirsty. Are those who persecuted the Protestants called Catholics? Should we call them Catholics? It would be much better to call them cannibals, for they behaved more like savages than Catholics or Christians in their bloody martyrdoms and murders of the saints of God.

In this age, we do not feel the cruelty of man to that extent, but this is only because the custom of the land will not allow it. There are many who dare not smite with the hand, but who are very busy in attacking with their tongue, and not by exposing our errors, which they have a perfect right to do – but in many cases the children of God are misrepresented, slandered, abused, persecuted, and ridiculed for truth's sake. We also know many instances where other methods are resorted to – anything to drive the servants of God away from their integrity and from their simple following of their Master. Well did the Lord Jesus say, *But keep yourselves from men* (Matthew 10:17), and *Behold, I send you forth as sheep in the midst of wolves; be ye therefore prudent as serpents and innocent as doves* (Matthew 10:16).

Do not expect others to be friends of your piety, or if they are, suspect the reality of that piety of which the ungodly man is a friend. You must expect to be sometimes bullied and sometimes coerced, to be sometimes flattered and sometimes threatened. You must expect at one time to meet with the flattering tongue that has under it the drawn sword, and at another time to meet with the drawn sword itself. Be aware, and expect that people will be against you. But what are they all? Suppose every living person in the world were against you and that you had to stand alone like Athanasius did in the fourth century. You could say, as Athanasius did, "I, Athanasius, against the whole world. I know I have truth on my side, and therefore against the world I stand."

**You must expect to be sometimes bullied and sometimes coerced, to be sometimes flattered and sometimes threatened.**

What use was the malice of men against Martin Luther? They wanted to burn him, but he died in his bed despite them all. They wanted to put an end to him, but his writings went everywhere, and the words of Luther seemed to be carried on the wings of angels, until in the most distant places, the pope found an enemy suddenly springing up where he thought the good seed had all been destroyed.

I don't know that it is of any very great service to have large numbers of people with you. Truth in general seems to be with the minority, and it is quite as honorable to serve God with two or three people as it would be with two or three million. If numbers or a majority made something right, idolatry would be the right religion. If in countries across the sea, numbers made something right, then those who fear the Lord would be few indeed, and idolatry and Romanism would be the right thing. Never judge according to numbers. They are nothing but people after all. If they are good people, then fight on their side, but if they and the truth are on opposing sides, do not join with them. Be a friend to the truth. Make your appeal *to the law and to the testimony! If they do not speak according to this word, it is because there is no light in them* (Isaiah 8:20).

That was splendid of Latimer, when he preached before Henry VIII. He had greatly displeased the king by his boldness in a sermon preached before the king, and was ordered to preach again on the following Sunday, and to apologize for the offense he had given. After reading his text, Bishop Latimer thus began his sermon: "Hugh Latimer, do you know before whom you are this day to speak? To the high and mighty monarch, the king's most excellent majesty, who can take away your life if you offend him. Therefore, take heed that you do not say anything that might displease him.

"But then consider well, Hugh, do you not know from where you come and upon whose message you are sent? Even by the great and mighty God, who is all-present, who beholds all your ways, and who is able to cast your soul into hell! Therefore, take care that you deliver your message faithfully."

Latimer then proceeded with the same sermon he had preached the preceding Sunday, but with considerably more energy. All God's children should show such courage when they are dealing with man. You are only a worm, but if God puts His truth into you, do not play the coward or stammer out His message, but stand up boldly for God and for His truth.

Some people are forever making excuses by what they call a decent humility. Humility is a good thing, but an ambassador of God must remember that there are other virtues besides humility. If the king sent an ambassador to a country with whom we were at war, and the little man were to step into the conference and say, "I humbly hope you will excuse my being here. I want to be in all things complacent to all of you lords and dignitaries. I am a young man, and you are much older than I am, and therefore I cheerfully submit my judgment to your superior wisdom and experience," and so on, then I am sure that the king would command him back again and command him into a long retirement. What business has he to humble himself when he is an ambassador for the king? He must remember that he is clothed with the dignity of the power that sent him.

This is how it is with God's messenger, and he considers it a vile shame to stoop to any man. He takes for his motto, *Cedo nulli*: "I yield to none," and preaching God's truth in love and honesty, he hopes to be able to give a good account to his Master at the end, for only unto his Master does he stand or fall.

# Chapter 22

# Be Faithful

*Well done, thou good and faithful slave; thou hast been faithful over a few things; I will set thee over many things; enter thou into the joy of thy lord.* (Matthew 25:21)

Here comes George Whitefield, the man who stood before twenty thousand people at a time to preach the gospel, who in England, Scotland, Ireland, and America has proclaimed the truth of God, and who could count his converts by thousands, even under one sermon! Here he comes, the man who endured persecution and scorn, and yet was not moved – the man of whom the world was not worthy, who lived for his fellow men, and who died at last for their cause. Stand by, angels, and admire, while the Master takes him by the hand and says, "Well done, well done, thou good and faithful servant; enter thou into the joy of thy Lord." See how free grace honors the man whom it enabled to do valiantly!

Look! Who is this who comes there? She is a poor, thin-looking creature, who on earth was weak and sick much of her life. She was often feverish and pale, and she lay three long years upon her bed of sickness. Was she a prince's daughter? For it seems heaven is making quite a stir about her.

No – she was a poor girl who earned her living by her needle, and she worked herself to death! Stitch, stitch, stitch from morning to night, and here she comes. She went prematurely to her grave, but she is coming, like a shock of corn fully ripe, into heaven, and her Master says, *Well done, thou good and faithful slave; thou hast been faithful over a few things; I will set thee over many things; enter thou into the joy of thy lord.*

She takes her place by the side of Whitefield. Ask her what she did, and you find out that she used to live in some back room, down some dark alley in the city. You will learn that there used to be another poor girl who would work with her, and that poor girl, when she first came to work with her, was a frivolous and lighthearted creature, and this weak child told her about Christ. When the sickly young lady was well enough to leave the room, they used to go to chapel or to church together in the evening.

It was hard at first to get the other one to go, but she used to urge her lovingly, and when the girl went wild a little, she never gave her up. She used to say, "O Jane, I wish you loved the Savior." When Jane was not there, she used to pray for her, and when she was there, she prayed with her. Every now and then when she was stitching away, she would read a page out of the Bible to her, for poor Jane could not read. With many tears, she tried to tell her about the Savior who loved her and gave Himself for her.

At last, after many days of difficult persuasion, many hours of sad disappointment, and many nights of sleepless, tearful prayer, she lived to see the girl profess her love to Christ. She then soon left her when her illness progressed, and there she lay until she was taken to the hospital, where she died. Even when she was in the hospital, she had a few tracts that she would give to those who came to see her. She would try, if she could, to get the women to come around, and she would give them a tract.

When she first went into the hospital, if she was able to get out of bed, she used to get by the side of someone who was dying and speak to them about Jesus Christ and eternity. When she became too ill to get out of bed, she used to ask a woman on the other side of the ward, who was getting better and was soon leaving the hospital, if she would come and read a chapter of the Bible to her. It was not that she wanted her to read to her on her own account, but for the woman's sake, for she thought it might affect her heart and mind while she was reading it.

At last, this poor girl died and fell asleep in Jesus, and she heard her Master say, "Well done." Nothing better could have been said to her, even by an archangel. *She has done what she could* (Mark 14:8).

See, then, the Master's commendation, and the last reward will be the same for all who have used their talents well. If there are any degrees in glory, they will not be distributed according to our talents, but according to our faithfulness in using them. As to whether there are degrees or not, I do not know, but this I know: he who does the will of the Lord Jesus will have it said to him, *Well done, thou good and faithful slave.*

# Chapter 23

# The Light of Evening

If our sun does not go down before it is noon, we may expect to have an evening time of life. Either we will be taken from this world by death, or else, if God should spare us, before long we will get to the evening of life. In a few more years, the dry and yellow leaf will be the fit companion of every man and woman. Is there anything sad in that? I do not think so. The time of old age, with all its infirmities, seems to me to be a time of special blessedness and privilege to the Christian. To the worldly sinner, whose appetite for pleasure has been removed by the frailty of his powers and the decay of his strength, old age must be a time of dullness and pain; but to the veteran soldier of the cross, old age must assuredly be a time of great joy and blessedness.

I was thinking the other evening, while riding in a delightful country, how similar to evening time old age is. The hot sun has gone down. That sun that shone upon that early piety of ours that did not have much depth of root and was scorched so that it died – that sun that next scorched our true godliness and often made it nearly wither, and would have withered it, had it not been planted by the rivers of water – that sun is now set.

The good old man has no particular care now in all the world. He says to business, to the hum, noise, and strife of the age in which he lives, "You are nothing to me. To make my calling and election sure, to hold firmly this my confidence, and to wait until my change comes – this is my duty now. I have no connection with all your worldly pleasures and cares."

The toil of his life is all done. He no longer needs to be sweating and toiling as he did in his youth and manhood. His family has grown up, and they are no longer dependent upon him. It may be that God has blessed him and he has sufficient provision for the needs of his old age, or it may be that in some rustic almshouse he breathes out the last few years of his existence. How calm and quiet! Like the laborer who, when he returns from the field in the evening, casts himself upon his couch, so does the old man rest from his labors. At evening time we gather into families, the fire is kindled, the curtains are drawn, and we sit around the family fire, to think no more of the things of the great rumbling world; and even then, in old age, the family, and not the world, is the engrossing topic.

Did you ever notice how respectable grandfathers, when they write a letter, fill it full of information concerning their children? "John is well," "Mary is sick," "Our family is in good health." It is very likely that some business might write to him and say, "Stocks are down," or "The interest rate has been raised," but you never find that in any of the good old man's letters. He writes about his family, his recently married daughters, and similar things. That is just what we do at evening time – we only think of the family circle, and we forget the world. That is what the gray-headed old man does. He thinks of his children and forgets about everything else.

Well, then, how sweet it is to think that for such an old man there is light in the darkness! *At evening time there shall be light* (Zechariah 14:7). Do not dread your days of weariness or your hours of decay. O soldier of the cross, new lights will burn when the old lights have gone out. New candles will be lit when the lamps of life are dim. Do not be afraid! The night of your decline may be coming on, but *at evening time there shall be light.*

At evening time, the Christian has many lights that he never had before – lights that are lit by the Holy Spirit and are shining by His light. There is the light of a bright experience. He can look back, and he can raise his Ebenezer saying, "Hither by thy help I've come."[11] He can look back at his old Bible, the light of his youth, and he can say, "This promise has been proved to me. This covenant has been proved true. I have read my Bible for many years, and I have never yet come across a broken promise. The promises have all been kept to me; not one good thing has failed." *There failed not a word of all the good things which the LORD had spoken unto the house of Israel; all of it came to pass* (Joshua 21:45).

Then, if he has served God, he has another light to cheer him: he has the light of the remembrance of the good that God has enabled him to do. Some of his spiritual children come in and talk of times when God blessed his conversation to their souls. He looks upon his children and his children's children, rising up to call the Redeemer blessed, and at evening time he has a light.

At last the night comes in real earnest. He has lived long enough, and he must die. The old man is on his bed. The sun is going down, and he has no more light. "Open up the windows and let me look for the last time into the open sky," says the old man. "The sun has gone down. I cannot see the mountains in

---

11    This is from the hymn "Come, Thou Fount of Every Blessing," by Robert Robinson (1735-1790). It is based upon 1 Samuel 7:12: *Then Samuel took a stone, and set it between Mizpeh and Shen, and called the name of it Ebenezer, saying, Hitherto hath the LORD helped us.*

the distance. They are all a mass of mist. My eyes are dim, and the world is dim too."

Suddenly, a light shoots across his face, and he cries, "O Daughter! Daughter, here! I can see another sun rising. Did you not tell me that the sun went down just now? Look, I see another! And where those hills used to be in the landscape, those hills that were lost in darkness, I can see hills that seem like burning brass, and I think that I can see upon that summit a city as bright as jasper. Yes, and I see a gate opening, and spirits coming forth. What is it that they say? Oh, they sing! They sing! Is this death?!"

And before he has asked the question, he has gone where he needs not to answer it, for death is unknown there. Yes, he has passed the gates of pearl. His feet are on the streets of gold. His head is adorned with the crown of immortality. The palm branch of eternal victory is in his hand. God has accepted him in the beloved. *To the praise of the glory of his grace, in which he has made us accepted in the beloved* (Ephesians 1:6).

# Chapter 24

# Beds That Are Too Short

For the bed is shorter than that a man can stretch himself on it: and the covering narrower than that he can wrap himself in it. (Isaiah 28:20)

As to the present world, there are many beds of man's own invention. One man has made himself a bedframe of gold. The posts of the bed are of silver. The covering thereof is of Tyrian purple. The pillows are filled with down, such as only much fine gold could buy him. The drapery is embroidered with threads of gold and silver, and they are drawn upon rings of ivory. This person has searched all over the earth for luxuries, and has had made for himself all manner of lavish delights. He acquires many acres of land and adds house to house and field to field. He digs, he toils, he labors, hoping that he will get enough, a sufficiency, a satisfactory inheritance. He proceeds from enterprise to enterprise. He invests his money in one sphere of labor and then another. He attempts to multiply his gold until it is more than can be counted. He becomes a merchant prince, a millionaire, and he says to himself, *Soul, thou hast many goods laid up for many years; take thine ease, eat, drink, and be merry* (Luke 12:19).

Do you not envy this man his situation? Are there not some of you whose only object in life is to do the same for yourselves? You say, "He has well-feathered his nest. I wish that I could do the same for myself!" Ah, but do you know that this bed is shorter than that he can stretch himself upon it? If you cast yourself upon it for a moment, you think that the bed is long enough for you, but it is not long enough for him.

I have often thought that many a man's riches would be sufficient for me, but they are not sufficient for him. If he makes them his god and seeks his happiness in them, you never find that the man has enough money. He still believes that his lands are too narrow and his estate is too small. When he begins to stretch himself, he finds there is something more needed. If the bed could only be made a little longer, then he thinks he could be satisfied and have enough room. But when the bed is lengthened, he finds that he has grown longer too. When his fortune has grown as big as the bedstead of Og, king of Bashan, even then he finds he cannot lie upon it easily. *For only Og, king of Bashan, had remained of the remnant of giants; behold, his bedstead was a bedstead of iron; is it not in Rabbath of the sons of Ammon? Nine cubits was the length thereof and four cubits the breadth of it, after the cubit of a man* (Deuteronomy 3:11).

We read of one man, Alexander, who stretched himself along the whole world that he had conquered, but he found there was not room, and he began to weep because there were no other worlds to conquer. One would have thought a little province would have been enough for him to rest in. Oh no – so big is man when he stretches himself that the whole world does not suffice him. No, but if God should give to the greedy all the mines of Peru, all the glittering diamonds of Golconda, India, and all the wealth of the world, and if he were then to transform the stars into gold and silver and make these greedy people emperors of an entire universe, even then the bed would not be long enough whereon they could stretch their ever-lengthening desires. The soul is wider than creation and broader than space. Even if these people were given everything, they would still be unsatisfied and would not find rest.

You say, "That is strange. If I had a little more, I would be very well satisfied." You make a mistake: if you are not content with what you have, you would not be satisfied if it were doubled.

"No," someone says, "I would be." You do not know yourself. If you have set your affection on the things of this world, that affection is like a horse leech; it cries, *Give, give* (Proverbs 30:15). It will suck, suck, suck to all eternity, and will still cry, *Give, give*; and though you give it all, it has not gotten enough. The bed is, in fact, *shorter than that a man can stretch himself on it.*

Let us look in another direction. Other people have said, "Well, I do not care for gold and silver. I thank God that I am not greedy." However, they have pursued fame and great success. "Oh," someone says, "what would I not do to be famous! If my name would be handed down to posterity as having done something and having been somebody, a person of importance, how satisfied would I be!"

And that person has so acted that he has at last made for himself a place of honor. He has become famous. There is hardly a newspaper that does not record his name. His name has become a household word. Nations listen to his voice. Thousands of trumpets proclaim his deeds. He is a man, and the world knows it and stamps him with the adjective "great." He is called a "great man." See how nice his situation is! What would some of you give to have the same! He breathes the breath of fame and smells the fragrance of applause. The world waits to refresh him with renewed flattery. Oh, would you not give your ears and eyes if you could be in a similar situation!

But did you ever read the history of famous people or hear them tell their story in secret? "Uneasy lies the head that wears the crown,"[12] even though it may be the laurel coronet of honor. When the person is known, you see that it is not enough; he asks for wider praise. There was a time when the admiration of a couple of old women was fame to him. Now the esteem of ten thousand is nothing. He talks of people as if they were but herds of wild donkeys, and what he looked up to once as a high pinnacle he now considers as beneath his feet.

He must go higher and higher and higher. Even though his head is reeling, his brain is whirling, and his feet are slipping, he must go higher. He has done great things, but he must do more. He seems to stride across the world, but thinks that he must leap further yet, for the world will never believe anyone to be famous unless he constantly outdoes himself. He must not only do a great thing today, but he must also do a greater thing tomorrow, and the next day a greater thing still. He must pile his mountains one upon another until he mounts the very Olympus of the demigods.

However, suppose he gets there. What does he say? "Oh, that I could go back to my cottage, that I might be unknown, that I might have rest with my family and have peace and quiet. Popularity is a care that I never endured until now. It is a trouble that I never guessed. Let me lose it all. Let me go back!" He is sick of it, for the fact is that we never can be satisfied with anything less than the approval of heaven, and until conscience gets that, all the applause of senators and princes would be a bed shorter than a man could stretch himself upon.

There is another bed on which man thinks he could rest. There is a sorceress, a painted harlot, who wears the richest gems in her ears and a necklace of precious things about her neck. She is an old deceiver. She was old and shriveled in the days of Bunyan. She decorated herself then, she does so now, and she will as long as the world endures. She roams around,

---

12    This quote is from William Shakespeare's *Henry IV* play.

and men think of her as young, fair, lovely, and desirable. Her name is Madam Licentious. She keeps a house wherein she feeds men and makes them drunk with the wine of pleasure, which is as honey to the taste, but is venom to the soul. This enchantress, when she can, entices men into her bed. "There," she says, "how daintily have I spread it!"

It is a bed, the pillars whereof are pleasure. Above is the purple of joy, and beneath is the soft serenity of luxurious self-indulgence. Oh, what a bed this is! Solomon once laid in it, and many since his time have sought their rest there. They have said, "Away with your gold and silver. Let me spend it, that I may eat, drink, and be merry, for tomorrow I die. Do not tell me about fame; I do not care for it. I would sooner have the pleasures of life or the joys of Bacchus than the glory of fame. Let me give myself up to the intoxication of this world's delights. Let me be drowned in the vat of wine of this world's joys."

Have you ever seen such men as that? I have seen many and have wept over them. I know some now. They are stretching themselves on that bed, trying to make themselves happy. Lord Byron is a picture of such men, though he outdid others. What a bed that was that he stretched himself on! Was ever a libertine more free in his sin? Was ever a sinner more wild in his blasphemy? Was ever a poet more daring in his flights of thought? Was ever anyone more injurious to his fellows than he?

Yet what did Byron say? There is a verse of his that tells you just what he felt in his heart. The man had all that he wanted of sinful pleasure, but here is his confession:

I fly, like a bird of the air,
In search of a home and a rest;
A balm for the sickness of care,
A bliss for a bosom unbless'd.[13]

13　This is a stanza from Lord Byron's poem "Farewell to England."

Yet he found it not. He had no rest in God. He tried pleasure until his eyes were red with it. He tried wickedness until his body was sick. He descended into his grave a premature old man. If you had asked him, and if he had spoken honestly, he would have said that the bed was shorter than that he could stretch himself upon it.

No, young man, you can have all the sin and all the pleasure and amusement of this world – and there is much to be found, of which I make no mention here – and when you have it all, you will find that it does not equal your expectation nor satisfy your desires. When the devil is bringing you one cup of spiced wine, you will be asking him next time to spice it more. He will flavor it to your fiery taste, but you will be dissatisfied still, until at last, if he were to bring you a cup as hot as damnation, it would fall tasteless on your palate. You would say, "Even this is tasteless to me, except in the pain, bitter wormwood, and fire that it brings."

It is this way with all worldly pleasure. There is no end to it. It is a perpetual thirst. It is like the opium addict. He eats a little, and he dreams such strange wonders; he wakes, and where are they? Such dreamers, when awake, look like dead men, with just enough life to enable them to crawl along. The next time, to get to their desired state, they must take more opium, and the next time more and more, and all the while they are gradually going down an inclined plane into their graves. That is simply the effect of human pleasure – and all worldly, carnal delights. They end only in destruction. Even while they last, they are not wide enough for our desire or large enough for our expectations, *for the bed is shorter than that a man can stretch himself on it.*

Now think for a moment of the Christian, and see the picture reversed. I will imagine the Christian at his very worst state, although there is no reason why I should do so. The Christian is not necessarily poor; he may be rich, but suppose he is poor. He has not a foot of land to call his own. He lives day by day, and he lives well, for his Master keeps a good cupboard for him and furnishes him with all he requires. He has nothing in this world except the promise of God with regard to the future. The worldly man laughs at the promise and says it is good for nothing.

Now look at the Christian. He says:

> There's nothing round this spacious globe,
>     Which suits my large desires;
> To nobler joys than nature gives,
> Thy servant, Lord, aspires.[14]

What, poor man – are you perfectly content? "Yes," he says. "It is my Father's will that I should live in poverty. I am perfectly content."

"But is there nothing else you wish for?"

"Nothing," he answers. "I have the presence of God. I have delight in communion with Christ. I know that there is laid up for me a crown of life that does not fade away, and there is nothing more that I could want. I am perfectly content. My soul is at rest."

From now on there is laid up for me a crown of righteousness, which the Lord, the righteous judge, shall give me at that day, and not to me only, but unto all those also that have loved his appearing. (2 Timothy 4:8)

When the great Prince of the pastors shall appear, ye shall receive the incorruptible crown of glory. (1 Peter 5:4)

---

14    This is a stanza adapted from a hymn by Philip Doddridge (1702-1751) found in a book published by Job Orton in 1755 from Doddridge's manuscript called *Hymns Founded on Various Texts in the Holy Scriptures*. It is based upon 2 Samuel 23:5: *Although my house be not so with God; yet he hath made with me an everlasting covenant, ordered in all things, and sure: for this is all my salvation, and all my desire, although he make it not to grow.*

# Chapter 25

# Mistaken Zeal

Those who have no life nor energy may easily ruin themselves, but they are not likely to harm others; but a mistaken zealot is like a madman with a torch in his hand. People who are zealous and also mistaken can do a whole lot of harm! Look at those scribes and Pharisees in Christ's day! They were very zealous, and under the pressure of their zeal they crucified the Lord of glory. What did Saul do in his time? He was very zealous, and under the influence of his zeal he dragged men and women to prison, tried to get them to blaspheme, and when they were put to death, he gave his voice against them.

I do not doubt that many who burned the martyrs were quite as sincere in their faith as those whom they burned. In fact, it must have taken an incredible amount of sincerity in the case of some to have been able to believe that the cruelties they practiced were really pleasing to God. We cannot doubt that they had such sincerity. Did not our Lord Himself say, *The hour will even come when whosoever kills you will think that he does God service* (John 16:2)?

Documents written by men who stained their hands with the blood of Protestants prove that some of them had a right heart toward God. In their mistaken zeal for God, truth, and church unity, they believed that they were crushing out a very deadly error, and that the people whom they sent to prison and to death were criminals who should have been exterminated because they were destroyers of the souls of men.

Be very careful that none of you fall into a persecuting spirit through your zeal for the gospel. A good woman might be intensely zealous, and for that reason she may say, "I will not have someone work in my house who does not go to my place of worship." I have known landlords, wonderfully zealous for the faith, who have therefore turned every Dissenter out of their houses and have refused to rent one of their farms to a Nonconformist.

I am not surprised by their conduct. If they are zealous, and at the same time blind, they will naturally take to exterminating the children of God. Of course, in their zeal they feel as if they must root out error and schism. They will not have Nonconformity near them, and so they get to work, and in their zeal, they hack right and left. They say strong things and bitter things, and then proceed to do cruel things – very cruel things – really believing that, in all that they do, they are doing God service.

They do not realize that they are violating the crown rights of God, who alone is Lord of the consciences of men. They would not oppose the will of God if they knew that they were doing so, and yet they are doing so. They would not willingly grieve the hearts of those whom God loves, and yet they do so when they are oppressing the humble cottager for his faith. They look upon the poor people who differ a little from them as being atrociously wrong, and they consider it to be their duty to set their faces against them. So, under the influence of the zeal that motivates them, which, in itself, is a good thing, they are led to do that which is sinful and unjust. Hence the apostle Paul, after he had felt the weight of the stones from the hands of the Jews, prayed that they might be saved – for if they were not saved, their zeal for God would continue to make murderers of them.

Another reason why we desire to see the zealous converted is because they would be so very useful. The person who is desperately earnest in a wrong way will be just as earnest in the right way – if you can just show him his wrong and teach him what is right. Oh, what splendid Christians some would make who are now such devotees of religion and tradition! Despite their inerrant beliefs, I look upon many religious churchgoers with admiration. They are up in the morning early, or late at night, ready to practice all kinds of mortifications, to give their very bodies to be burned, to give away their possessions in alms, ready to offer prayers without number,

> The person who is desperately earnest in a wrong way will be just as earnest in the right way – if you can just show him his wrong and teach him what is right.

and to be obedient to rites and ceremonies without end. What more could external religion demand of mortal men? Oh, if we could get these to sit at Jesus' feet, leave the phylacteries and the broad-bordered garments, worship God in spirit, and have no confidence in the flesh, what wonderful Christians they would make! *But they do all their works that they may be seen of men: they make broad their phylacteries and enlarge the borders of their garments* (Matthew 23:5).

See what Paul himself was, when, counting all he had valued so dear to be but dung, he left it all behind and began to preach salvation by grace alone.

I even count all things as loss for the excellency of the knowledge of Christ Jesus my Lord, for whom I have suffered the loss of all things and do count them but dung, that I may win Christ and be found in him, not having my own righteousness, which is of the law, but that which is through the faith of Christ, the righteousness which is of God by faith. (Philippians 3:8-9)

While Paul traveled over the world like a lightning flash and preached the gospel as with a peal of thunder, he loved, lived, and died for the Nazarene, whom once in his zeal he had considered to be an impostor. People should pray with all their might for those people who are zealous but mistaken, who *have a zeal of God, but not according to knowledge* (Romans 10:2).

We are bound to make these people the subject of especially earnest prayer because it is so difficult to convert them. It really requires the power of God to convert anybody, but there seems to be a double manifestation of power in the conversion of a downright bigot when his bigotry is associated with dense ignorance and glaring error.

"Oh," he says, "I do that which is right. I am strict in my religion. My righteousness will save me." You cannot get him to stop believing that. It is easier to get a sinner out of his sin than a self-righteous person out of his self-righteousness. Conceit of our own righteousness sticks to us as the skin to the flesh. A leopard can sooner lose his spots than the proud man his self-righteousness. Oh, that righteousness of ours! We are so fond of it. Our pride hugs it. We do so much like to think that we are good, upright, true, and right in the sight of God by nature – and though we are beaten out of that belief with many stripes, yet our tendency is always to return to it.

Self-righteousness is bound up in the heart of a man as folly in the heart of a child (Proverbs 22:15). *Though thou should bray a fool in a mortar among wheat with a pestle*, yet his self-righteous folly will not depart from him (Proverbs 27:22). He will hold on to his belief that, after all, he is a good person and deserves to be saved. We must, therefore, in a very special manner pray for such people, knowing that self-righteousness is a deep ditch and that it is hard to draw those people out once they have fallen into it.

Prejudice – preconceived opinions that are not based upon truth or reason – of all other opponents, is one of the worst to overcome. The door is locked. You can knock as long as you like, but the man will not open it. He cannot. It is locked, and he has thrown away the key. You may tell him, "You are wrong, good friend," but he is so comfortably assured that he is right that your explanation and reasoning will only make him more angry at you for attempting to disturb his peace.

*O God! Who but You can draw a person out of this miry clay of self-righteousness? Therefore do we cry to You, of Your great grace, to do it.*

For these and many other reasons, those who have a zeal for God, but not according to knowledge, must have an essential place in our unrelenting prayers.

# Chapter 26

# Selfish Ease

Selfish ease is the sin about which the Spirit of God says by Moses, *Be sure your sin will catch up with you* (Numbers 32:23). One educated clergyman has preached a sermon on the sin of murder from this text, another sermon about theft, and another about falsehood. They are very good sermons, but they have nothing to do with this text, if it is read as Moses uttered it. If you take the text as it stands, there is nothing in it about murder or theft or anything of the kind. In fact, it is not about what people do, but it is about what people do not do. The iniquity of doing nothing is a sin that is not so often spoken of as it should be. A sin of omission is clearly aimed at in this warning: *If ye will not do so, behold, ye shall have sinned against the LORD, and be sure your sin will catch up with you.*

What was this sin, then? Remember that it is the sin of God's own people. It is not the sin of the Egyptians and Philistines, but the sin of God's chosen nation. Therefore, this text is for you who belong to any of the tribes of Israel – you to whom God has given a portion among His beloved ones. It is to you, professed Christians and church members, that the text comes: *Be sure your sin will catch up with you.*

What is that sin? Very sadly, it is common among professed Christians and needs to be dealt with. It is the sin that leads many to forget their place in the holy war that is to be carried out for God and for His church. A great many wrongs are tangled together in this crime, and we must try to separate them and set them in order before our eyes.

First, it was the sin of idleness and of self-indulgence. The tribes of Reuben, Gad, and half of Manasseh wanted to remain on this side of the Jordan River rather than enter the promised land. "We have cattle, and here is a land that yields much pasture. Let us have this for our cattle, and we will build folds for our sheep with the abundant stones that lie about. We will rebuild these cities of the Amorites, and we will live in them. They are nearly ready for us, and there our little ones will dwell in comfort. We do not care about fighting. We have seen enough of it already in the wars with Sihon and Og. Reuben would rather abide by the sheepfolds. Gad has more delight in the bleating of the sheep and in the folding of the lambs in his bosom than in going forth to battle" (Numbers 32).

The tribe of Reuben is not dead; the tribe of Gad has not passed away! Many are still like that today. Many who are of the household of faith are equally disinclined to exertion and are equally fond of ease. Hear them say, "Thank God we are safe! We have passed from death unto life. We have named the name of Christ. We are washed in His precious blood, and therefore we are secure."

Then, with a strange inconsistency, they allow the evil of the flesh to crave carnal ease, and they cry, *Soul, thou hast many goods laid up for many years; take thine ease, eat, drink, and be merry* (Luke 12:19). Spiritual self-indulgence is a monstrous evil, yet we see it all around. On Sunday these loafers want to be well fed. They look for sermons that will feed their souls. The thought does not occur to these people that there is something else to be done besides feeding.

Saving souls is pushed into the background. The crowds are perishing at their gates. The multitudes with their sins defile the air. The age is getting worse and worse and mankind is becoming more and more evil, yet these people want pleasant things preached to them. They eat the fat and drink the sweet, and they crowd to the feast of contentment, amusement, and ease. Spiritual festivals are their delight. They seek seminars, conferences, and emotional entertainment, but they do not want earnest prayer and convicting sermons.

> The age is getting worse and worse and mankind is becoming more and more evil, yet these people want pleasant things preached to them.

They do not want anything that involves effort, work, or sacrifice. They do not put on any armor. They grasp no sword, they wield no sling, and they throw no stone. No, they have gotten what they want. They go to church and think they are on their way to heaven, and they sit down in carnal security, satisfied to do nothing. They neither work for life, nor from life. They are utter sluggards, as lazy as they are long. Nowhere are they at home except where they can enjoy themselves and take things easy. They love their beds, but they will neither plow nor reap the Lord's fields.

This is the sin pointed out in the text: if you do not go forth to the battles of the Lord and contend for the Lord God and for His people, you sin against the Lord – *and be sure your sin will catch up with you.* The sin of doing nothing is about the biggest of all sins, for it involves most other sins. The sin of sitting still while your brethren go forth to war breaks both tables of the law and has in it a huge idolatry of self, which neither allows love to God or to others. Horrible idleness! God save us from it!

# Chapter 27

# Be Sober

*B*e *temperate [sober]* (1 Peter 1:13; 5:8). Be serious-minded, sensible, solemn, steady, thoughtful, and earnest. That means to show moderation in all things. Do not be so excited with joy as to become childish. Do not grow intoxicated and delirious with worldly gain or honor. On the other hand, do not be too much depressed with passing troubles. There are some who are so far from moderation that if a little goes wrong with them, they are ready to cry, "Let me die!" No, no.

*Be temperate.* Be clearheaded. Keep on the narrow path. There are many people to whom this exhortation is most needful. Are there not people around us who blow hot today and cold tomorrow? Their heat is scorching and their cold is frigid. You might think they were angels from the way they talk one day, but you might think them angels of another sort from the way they act at other times. They are either so high up or so low down that in either case they are extreme. Today they are carried away with this, and the next day they are carried away with that.

I knew a Christian man very well to whom I was accustomed to use one specific greeting whenever I saw him. He was a good man, but changeable. I said to him, "Good morning, friend! What are you now?" He was one time a valiant Arminian, setting young people right as to the errors of my Calvinistic teaching. A short time later, he became exceedingly Calvinistic himself and wanted to lift me up several degrees higher, but I declined to yield. Soon he became a Baptist, and he agreed with me on all points, as far as I know. This was not good enough, and therefore he became a Plymouth Brethren. After that, he went back to the church from which he originally started.

When I next met him, I said, "Good morning, brother. What are you now?"

He replied, "That is too bad, Mr. Spurgeon; you asked me the same question last time."

I replied, "Did I? But what are you now? Will the same answer do?"

I knew it would not. I would earnestly say to all such brethren, "Be sober. Be sober." It cannot be wise to stagger all over the road in this way. Make sure of your footing when you stand; make doubly sure of it before you shift.

To be sober (*temperate*) means to have a calm, clear head, to judge things after the rule of right and not according to the rule of mob. Do not be influenced by those who cry loudest in the street or by those who beat the biggest drum. Judge for yourselves as people of understanding. Judge as in the sight of God with calm deliberation.

*Be temperate.* That is, be clearheaded. The person who drinks, and thus destroys the sobriety of his body, is confused and muddled and has lost his way. Ceasing to be sober, he makes a fool of himself. Do not commit this sin spiritually. Be especially clearheaded and calm as to the things of God. Ask that the grace of God may so rule in your heart that you may be peaceful and serene and not troubled with groundless fear on one side or with foolish hope on the other.

*Be temperate*, says the apostle. The words translated as *be temperate* sometimes mean "be watchful," and indeed there is much in common between the two things. Live with your eyes open; do not go around half asleep. Many Christians are asleep. Whole congregations are asleep. The minister snores theology, and the people in the pews nod in chorus. Much sacred work is done in a sleepy style. You can have a Sunday school, and teachers and children can be asleep. You can have a tract-distributing society with visitors going around to the doors all asleep. You can do everything in a lethargic way if you want to. But the apostle Paul says be watchful, be alive. Brethren, look alive. Be so awakened by these fine arguments with which we have provided you already that you will brace yourselves up and throw your whole strength into the service of your Lord and Master.

> Live with your eyes open; do not go around half asleep.

Finally, let us *hope to the end. Therefore, having the loins of your understanding girded with temperance, wait perfectly in the grace that is presented unto you when Jesus, the Christ, is manifested unto you* (1 Peter 1:13). Never despair. Never even doubt. Hope when things look hopeless. A sick and suffering brother rebuked me the other day for being downcast. He said to me, "We should never display a lack of courage, but I think you do sometimes."

I asked him what he meant, and he replied, "You sometimes seem to grow despondent and gloomy. I am about to die, but I have no clouds and no fears."

I rejoiced to see him so joyous, and I answered, "That is right, my brother. Blame me as much as you want for my unbelief. I richly deserve it."

"You are the father of many of us," he said. "Did you not bring me and my friend over there to Christ? If you get low in spirit after so much blessing, you ought to be ashamed of yourself."

I could say nothing other than, "I am ashamed of myself, and I desire to be more confident in the future."

Brethren, we must hope and not fear. Be strong in holy confidence in God's Word, and be sure that His cause will live and prosper. Hope, says the apostle. Hope to the end. Go right on through with it. If the worst comes to the worst, hope still. Hope as much as ever a person can hope, for when your hope is in God, you cannot hope too much.

The hope shall not be ashamed, because the love of God is poured out in our hearts by the Holy Spirit which is given unto us. (Romans 5:5)

And believing, the God of hope fills you with all joy and peace that ye may abound in hope by the virtue of the Holy Spirit. (Romans 15:13)

# Chapter 28

# Through Floods and Flames

There are many dear children, both boys and girls, who have not been ashamed in their early days to come forward and confess the Lord Jesus Christ. God bless the dear children! I rejoice in them. I am sure that the church will never have to be ashamed of having admitted them. They, at least, show no cowardice. They are pleased in being numbered with the people of God, and they consider it an honor to be associated with Christ and His people.

Shame on you older ones who still hold back! What troubles you that children are braver than you? By the love you bear to Christ, I exhort you to come forth and confess His name among this evil and perverse generation!

Is it true? Then joyfully accept the trial that comes from it. Do not retreat from the flames. Settle it in your minds that, by divine grace, no loss, cross, shame, or suffering will make you play the coward. Say, like the holy children – Shadrach, Meshach, and Abednego – *We are not careful to answer thee in this matter* (Daniel 3:16). They did not cower before the king and cry, "We beg you not to throw us into the fiery furnace! Let us have a discussion with you, O king, that we may arrange some terms and conditions. There may be some way that we can please you and still keep our religion."

No. They said, *We are not careful to answer thee in this matter. Behold, our God whom we serve is able to deliver us from the burning fiery furnace, and he will deliver us out of thine hand, O king. But if not, be it known unto thee, O king, that we will not worship thy god, nor honour the statue which thou hast raised up* (Daniel 3:16-18).

Dear friends, let us be ready to suffer for Christ's sake. Some will say, "Do not be imprudent." It is always prudent to do your duty. We do not have enough nowadays of the virtue called imprudence. I would like to see a display of old-fashioned imprudence in these cold, calculating, selfish days. Oh, for the days of zeal, the days when people counted not their lives dear to them that they might win Christ! *None of these things move me, neither do I count my life dear unto myself, only that I might finish my course with joy and the ministry, which I have received of the Lord Jesus, to testify the gospel of the grace of God* (Acts 20:24).

> We do not have enough nowadays of the virtue called imprudence.

People sit down and figure out what it will cost them to do right, weighing their conduct as a matter of profit and loss, and then they call such wicked calculations prudence. It is utter selfishness. Do what is right, even if it costs you your life. Where would England have been if the men who won our liberties in former ages had negotiated with the world for gain? If they had saved their skins, they would have lost their souls – and would have ruined the cause of God in England. He who does not love Christ more than all things does not love Him. Oh, for men and women of principle, who consider nothing as loss but loss of faith, and desire no gain except the glory of God!

Let this be your cry:

Through floods and flames, if Jesus lead,
I'll follow where he goes.[15]

You may lose a great deal *for* Christ, but you will never lose anything *by* Christ. You may lose for time, but you will gain for eternity. The loss is only for a short while, but the gain is everlasting. You will gain by Christ, even if you have to go to heaven by the way of persecution, poverty, and slander. Never mind the way; the end will make full amends. The treasures of Egypt are mere rubbish compared with the riches of endless delight.

If it is true that you are willing to fully follow Christ, then you can count upon being rescued. Nebuchadnezzar may put you into the fire, but he cannot keep you there, nor can he make the fire burn you. The Enemy casts you bound into the fire, but the fire will loosen your bonds, and you will walk at liberty amid the glowing coals. You will gain by your losses. You will rise by being cast down.

Many prosperous people owe their success to the fact that they were faithful when they were in humble employments. They were honest, and for the moment they might have displeased their employers, but in the end they earned their esteem. When Adam Clarke[16] was an apprentice, and his master showed him how to stretch the cloth when it was a little short, Adam could not find it in his heart to do so. Such a fool of a boy must be sent home to his mother, and his godly mother was glad that her boy was such a fool that he could not stoop to a dishonest trick.

You know what he became. He might have missed his way in life if he had not been true to his principles in his youth. Your first loss may be a lifelong gain. Dear young fellow, you

---

15  This is from the hymn "In All My Lord's Appointed Ways" by Baptist pastor John Ryland (1753-1825).

16  Adam Clarke (1762-1832) was a Methodist preacher and theologian, best known for his biblical commentaries.

might lose a job or friends, but the Lord will turn the curse into a blessing. If all would go easily with you, you might decline in character, and by doing a little wrong, you might learn to do yet more and more wrong, and so lose your integrity, and with it all hope of ever advancing in life. Do right for the sake of Jesus Christ, without considering any consequences, and the consequences will be right and heaven-sent.

# Chapter 29

# Show Your Colors

The fact is that our Lord requires an open confession as well as a secret faith. If you will not give it, there is no promise of salvation for you, but instead a threat of being denied in the end. The apostle Paul puts it this way: *That if thou shalt confess with thy mouth the Lord Jesus and shalt believe in thine heart that God has raised him from the dead, thou shalt be saved* (Romans 10:9). It is stated in another place like this: *He that believes and is baptized shall be saved* (Mark 16:16). That is Christ's way of making our confession of Him.

If there is a true faith, there must be a declaration of it. If you are a candle, and God has lit you, then *let your light so shine before men that they may see your good works and glorify your Father who is in the heavens* (Matthew 5:16). Soldiers of Christ must, like soldiers of our nation, wear their uniforms; and if they are ashamed of their uniforms, they ought to be drummed out of the army. They are not honest soldiers who refuse to march in rank with their comrades.

The very least thing that the Lord Jesus Christ can expect of us is that we confess Him to the best of our power. If you are nailed up to a cross, I will not invite you to be baptized. If you are fastened to a tree to die, I will not ask you to go into a pulpit and declare your faith, for you cannot. But you are required to do what you can do, and that is to make as distinct and open a confession of the Lord Jesus Christ as may be suitable in your present condition.

I believe that many Christians get into a lot of trouble by not being honest in their convictions. For instance, if a person goes into a workshop, or a soldier into a barracks, and if he does not fly his flag from the beginning, it will be very difficult for him to run it up afterwards. But if he immediately and boldly lets them know, "I am a Christian, and there are certain things that I cannot do to please you, and certain other things that I cannot help doing even though they might displease you" – when that is clearly understood, after a while the peculiarity of the thing will be gone, and the person will be let alone.

However, if he is a little dishonest and thinks that he is going to please the world and please Christ too, he can depend on it that he is in for a rough time. If he tries the way of compromise, his life will be like that of a toad under a harrow or a fox in a dog kennel. That will never do. Come out. Show your colors. Let it be known who you are and what you are. Although your course will not be smooth, it will certainly not be half as rough as if you tried to run with the hare and hunt with the hounds, which is a very difficult piece of business.

The man on the cross made his declaration then and there, and made as open a confession of his faith in Christ as was possible. The next thing he did was to rebuke his fellow sinner. He spoke to him in answer to the irreverence with which he had assailed our Lord. I do not know what the unconverted convict had been blasphemously saying, but his converted comrade spoke very honestly to him: *Dost not thou fear God, seeing thou art in the same condemnation? And we indeed justly, for we receive the due reward of our deeds; but this man has done nothing amiss* (Luke 23:40-41).

It is more than ever needful in these days that believers in Christ do not allow sin to go unrebuked, and yet a great many of them do so. Do you not know that a person who is silent when a wrong thing is said or done has become a participant in the sin? *When I say unto the wicked, O wicked man, thou shalt surely die; if thou dost not speak to warn the wicked from his way, that wicked man shall die for his sin; but I will require his blood at thine hand* (Ezekiel 33:8). If you do not rebuke sin – I mean, of course, on all suitable occasions and in a proper spirit – your silence will give consent to the sin, and you will be encouraging and supporting the sin.

> A person who saw a robbery and who did not yell, "Stop, thief!" would be thought to be associated with the thief.

A person who saw a robbery and who did not yell, "Stop, thief!" would be thought to be associated with the thief. The person who can hear swearing or see impurity and never utter a word of protest may well question whether he is righteous himself. Our "other people's sins" make up a large part of our personal guilt unless we rebuke them in their sins in some way. Our Lord expects us to do this. The dying thief did it, and he did it with all his heart, and in doing so he far exceeded large numbers of people who hold their heads high in the church but who should be ashamed at being silent regarding sin.

# Chapter 30

# Keep Your Own Garden

*B*e thou diligent to know the countenance of thy sheep, and *put thy heart into thy herds* (Proverbs 27:23). It is good for a man to see to his cattle and to look after his flocks and his herds, but he should not forget to cultivate that little patch of ground that lies in the center of his being. Let him educate his head and try to gain all knowledge, but let him not forget that there is another plot of ground called the heart – the character – which is more important still.

Right principles are spiritual gold, and he who has them and is ruled by them is the person who truly lives. No matter what else a person has, he who does not have his heart cultivated and made right and pure does not have life.

Have you ever thought about your own heart? I do not mean whether you have palpitations. I am no doctor. I am speaking now about the heart in its moral and spiritual aspect. What is your character, and do you seek to cultivate it? Do you ever use the hoe upon those weeds that are so plentiful in us all? Do you water those tiny plants of goodness that have begun to grow? Do you watch them to keep away the little foxes that would destroy them? Are you hopeful that there may yet be a harvest in your character that God will look upon with approval?

I pray that we may all look to our hearts. *Above all else, guard thy heart; for out of it flows the issues of life* (Proverbs 4:23). Pray daily, *Create in me a clean heart, O God, and renew a right spirit within me* (Psalm 51:10). If you do not, you will go up and down in the world and do a great deal, and when it comes to the end, you will find that you have neglected your noblest nature, and your poor starved soul will die that second death, which is the more dreadful because it is everlasting death. *Hades and death were cast into the lake of fire. This is the second death. And whosoever was not found written in the book of life was cast into the lake of fire* (Revelation 20:14-15).

How terrible for a soul to die of neglect! *How will we escape if we neglect so great a salvation* (Hebrews 2:3 NASB)? If we pay attention to our bodies, but not to our immortal souls, how can we justify our foolishness? May God save us from suicide by neglect! May we not have to moan out eternally, *They made me the keeper of the vineyards, but I have not kept mine own vineyard* (Song of Solomon 1:6).

Now consider another point and think of another vineyard. Are not some people neglecting their families? Next to our hearts, our households are the vineyards that we are most obligated to cultivate. I will never forget a man whom I knew in my youth who used to accompany me at times in my walks to the villages to preach. He was always willing to go with me any evening, but I did not need to ask him, for he asked himself – until I purposely stopped him from it.

He liked to hear himself preach much better than others liked to hear him, and he was a man who was sure to be somewhere in front of others if he could. Even if you snuffed him out, he had a way of lighting himself up again. He was good-natured and unable to be restrained. He was, I believe, sincerely earnest in doing good, but two boys of his were well-known to me, and they would swear horribly. They were ready for every sin and were under no restraint.

One of them drank himself into a dying state with brandy, although he was a mere boy. I do not believe his father had ever spoken to him about the habit of intoxication, although he certainly was sober and virtuous himself. I had no fault to find with him except this grave fault – that he was seldom at home, was not the leader of his house, and could not control his children. Neither husband nor wife occupied any place of influence in the household; they were simply the servants of their children. Their children made themselves vile, and they did not restrain them!

> If any of you have children and do not know where they are, go quickly and find out.

This man would pray for his children at the prayer meeting, but I don't think he ever practiced family prayer. It is shocking to find men and women speaking fluently about religion, and yet their houses are a disgrace to Christianity. I suppose that none of you are as bad as that, but if you are, please think this text over: *They made me the keeper of the vineyards, but I have not kept mine own vineyard.*

The most careful and prayerful father cannot be held accountable for having wicked sons if he has done his best to instruct them in the ways of God. The most concerned and tearful mother cannot be blamed if her daughter dishonors the family, as long as her mother has done her best to train her up to be a godly and holy woman. But if the parents cannot say that they have done their best, and their children go astray, then they are at fault.

If any of you have children and do not know where they are, go quickly and find out. If any of you parents do not practice discipline nor seek to bring your children to Christ, I urge you to give up every kind of public work until you have first done your work at home.

Sir, has anybody made you a minister, and you are not trying to save your own children? I tell you, then, that I do not believe that God made you a minister, for if He had, He would have begun by making you a minister to your own family. *They made me the keeper of the vineyards.* "They" ought to have known better, and you ought to have known better than to accept the call. How can you be a steward in the great household of the Lord when you cannot even rule your own house?

Are you a Sunday school teacher, teaching other people's children, but never praying with your own? Is that not sad? Are you a teacher of a large class of youths who has never taught his own sons and daughters? What will you do when you see your children plunge into vice and sin, and you remember that you utterly neglected their souls?

I know not where this knife may cut, but if it wounds, please do not blunt its edge. Do you say that this is very personal? It is meant to be personal – and if anybody is offended by it, let him be offended with himself and mend his ways. No longer let this be true of any of us: *They made me the keeper of the vineyards, but I have not kept mine own vineyard.*

# Chapter 31

# A Talk about Death

It is the part of a brave person, and especially of one who believes in Jesus Christ, neither to dread death nor to long for it – neither to fear it nor to seek it. He should patiently possess his soul. He should not despair of life at simple trials, and he should always be more eager to run his race well than to reach its end.

It is no work of people of faith to predict their own deaths. These things are left to God. We do not know how long we will live on earth, and we do not need to know. We do not get to decide whether we have a short or a long life – and if we had such a choice, it would be wise for us to refer it back to our God. *Father, into thy hands I commend my spirit* (Luke 23:46) is an admirable prayer for living saints as well as for dying saints. To desire to pry between the folded leaves of the book of destiny is to desire a questionable privilege. We undoubtedly live better because we cannot foresee the moment when this life will reach its end.

Job made a mistake as to the date of his death, but he made no mistake as to the fact itself. He spoke truly when he said, *For I know that thou dost conduct me unto death* (Job 30:23).

Some day or other the Lord will call us from our home above ground to the house appointed for all living. I invite you now to consider this unquestioned truth. Do you hesitate? Why? Is it not very wise to talk about our last hours?

You say that you want to discuss something cheerful. Do you? Is this not a cheerful theme to you? It is a serious topic, but it also ought to be welcome to you. You say that you cannot stand the thought of death. Then you greatly need to think about it. Wanting to avoid it proves that you are not in a proper state of mind, or else you would take it into due consideration without reluctance.

It is a poor happiness that overlooks the most important of facts. I would not want a kind of peace that could only be maintained by thoughtlessness. You have something still to learn if you are a Christian and yet are not prepared to die. You need to reach a higher state of grace and attain to a firmer and more forceful faith. That you are still a babe in grace is clear from your admission that to depart and be with Christ does not seem to be a better thing for you than to abide in the flesh (Philippians 1:23).

Should it not be the business of this life to prepare for the next life and, in that respect, to prepare to die? But how can a person be prepared for that which he never thinks of? Do you intend to take a leap in the dark? If so, you are in an unhappy condition, and I implore you as you love your own soul to escape from such peril by the help of God's Holy Spirit.

"Oh," someone says, "but I do not feel called upon to think of it." Why, the very autumn of the year calls you to it. Each fading leaf admonishes you. You will most certainly have to die; why not think about the inevitable? It is said that the ostrich buries its head in the sand and imagines itself secure when it can no longer see the hunter. I can hardly imagine that even a bird could be quite so foolish, and I implore you not to take part in such foolishness.

If I do not think about death, death will still think about me. If I will not meditate upon and consider death, death will still come to me. Let me, then, meet it bravely and look it in the face. Death comes into our houses and takes away our loved ones. Seldom do I enter the pulpit without missing some familiar face from its place. Not a week passes by without some of our happy fellowship being caught away to the still-happier fellowship above. Whether we will hear him or not, death is preaching to us each time we assemble in public. Does he come so often with God's message and will we refuse to hear? No, but let us lend a willing ear and heart, and let us hear what the Lord God would say to us at all times.

> If I do not think about death, death will still think about me.

Oh, you who are youngest, you who are fullest of health and strength, I lovingly invite you not to put away this subject from you. Remember, the youngest may be taken away. When my own boys were young, I took them to the old churchyard of Wimbledon and directed them to look at some of the little graves there, and they found several whose lives were shorter than their own. I tried in this way to impress upon their young minds the uncertainty of life. I want every child to remember that he is not too young to die.

Let others know that they are not too strong to die. The sturdiest trees of the forest are often the first to fall beneath the destroyer's ax. Paracelsus, the renowned physician of old time, prepared a medicine of which he said that if a man took it regularly, he could never die, unless it were of extreme old age; yet Paracelsus himself died a young man. Those who think they have found the secret of immortality will learn that they are under a strong delusion. None of us can discover a spot where we are out of bowshot of the last enemy, and therefore it would be foolish to refuse to think of it.

A certain exceedingly arrogant French duke forbade his attendants ever to mention death in his hearing. When his secretary read to him the words, "The late king of Spain," the duke turned to him with scathing indignation and asked him what he meant by it. The poor secretary could only stammer out, "It is a title that they take."

Yes, indeed, it is a title we will all take, and it would be good to note how it will suit us. Death, the king of terrors, comes to kings, and he also visits paupers. He comes to you, to me, and to all. Let us all be ready for his certain arrival. Are you ready?

In a moment, in the twinkling of an eye, at the last trumpet, for the trumpet shall sound, and the dead shall be raised without corruption, and we shall be changed. For this corruptible must put on incorruption, and this mortal must put on immortality. So when this corruptible shall have put on incorruption, and this mortal shall have put on immortality, then shall be brought to pass the word that is written, Death is swallowed up in victory. O death, where is thy sting? O Hades, where is thy victory? The sting of death is sin, and the power of sin is the law. But thanks be to God, who gives us the victory through our Lord Jesus Christ. Therefore, my beloved brothers, be ye steadfast, unmovable, always abounding in the work of the Lord, forasmuch as ye know that your labour is not in vain in the Lord. (1 Corinthians 15:52-58)

# Charles H. Spurgeon –
# A Brief Biography

Charles Haddon Spurgeon was born on June 19, 1834, in Kelvedon, Essex, England. He was one of seventeen children in his family (nine of whom died in infancy). His father and grandfather were Nonconformist ministers in England. Due to economic difficulties, eighteen-month-old Charles was sent to live with his grandfather, who helped teach Charles the ways of God. Later in life, Charles remembered looking at the pictures in *Pilgrim's Progress* and in *Foxe's Book of Martyrs* as a young boy.

Charles did not have much of a formal education and never went to college. He read much throughout his life though, especially books by Puritan authors.

Even with godly parents and grandparents, young Charles

resisted giving in to God. It was not until he was fifteen years old that he was born again. He was on his way to his usual church, but when a heavy snowstorm prevented him from getting there, he turned in at a little Primitive Methodist chapel. Though there were only about fifteen people in attendance, the preacher spoke from Isaiah 45:22: *Look unto me, and be ye saved, all the ends of the earth.* Charles Spurgeon's eyes were opened and the Lord converted his soul.

He began attending a Baptist church and teaching Sunday school. He soon preached his first sermon, and then when he was sixteen years old, he became the pastor of a small Baptist church in Cambridge. The church soon grew to over four hundred people, and Charles Spurgeon, at the age of nineteen, moved on to become the pastor of the New Park Street Church in London. The church grew from a few hundred attenders to a few thousand. They built an addition to the church, but still needed more room to accommodate the congregation. The Metropolitan Tabernacle was built in London in 1861, seating more than 5,000 people. Pastor Spurgeon preached the simple message of the cross, and thereby attracted many people who wanted to hear God's Word preached in the power of the Holy Spirit.

On January 9, 1856, Charles married Susannah Thompson. They had twin boys, Charles and Thomas. Charles and Susannah loved each other deeply, even amidst the difficulties and troubles that they faced in life, including health problems. They helped each other spiritually, and often together read the writings of Jonathan Edwards, Richard Baxter, and other Puritan writers.

Charles Spurgeon was a friend of all Christians, but he stood firmly on the Scriptures, and it didn't please all who heard him. Spurgeon believed in and preached on the sovereignty of God, heaven and hell, repentance, revival, holiness, salvation through Jesus Christ alone, and the infallibility and necessity of the Word of God. He spoke against worldliness and hypocrisy among Christians, and against Roman Catholicism, ritualism, and modernism.

One of the biggest controversies in his life was known as the "Down-Grade Controversy." Charles Spurgeon believed that some pastors of his time were "down-grading" the faith by compromising with the world or the new ideas of the age. He said that some pastors were denying the inspiration of the Bible, salvation by faith alone, and the truth of the Bible in other areas, such as creation. Many pastors who believed what Spurgeon condemned were not happy about this, and Spurgeon eventually resigned from the Baptist Union.

Despite some difficulties, Spurgeon became known as the "Prince of Preachers." He opposed slavery, started a pastors' college, opened an orphanage, led in helping feed and clothe the poor, had a book fund for pastors who could not afford books, and more.

Charles Spurgeon remains one of the most published preachers in history. His sermons were printed each week (even in the newspapers), and then the sermons for the year were re-issued as a book at the end of the year. The first six volumes, from 1855-1860, are known as *The Park Street Pulpit*, while the next fifty-seven volumes, from 1861-1917 (his sermons continued to be published long after his death), are known as *The Metropolitan Tabernacle Pulpit*. He also oversaw a monthly magazine-type publication called *The Sword and the Trowel*, and Spurgeon wrote many books, including *Lectures to My Students, All of Grace, Around the Wicket Gate, Advice for Seekers, John Ploughman's Talks, The Soul Winner, Words of Counsel for Christian Workers, Cheque Book of the Bank of Faith, Morning and Evening*, his autobiography, and more, including some commentaries, such as his twenty-year study on the Psalms – *The Treasury of David*.

Charles Spurgeon often preached ten times a week, preaching

to an estimated ten million people during his lifetime. He usually preached from only one page of notes, and often from just an outline. He read about six books each week. During his lifetime, he had read *The Pilgrim's Progress* through more than one hundred times. When he died, his personal library consisted of more than 12,000 books. However, the Bible always remained the most important book to him.

Spurgeon was able to do what he did in the power of God's Holy Spirit because he followed his own advice – he met with God every morning before meeting with others, and he continued in communion with God throughout the day.

Charles Spurgeon suffered from gout, rheumatism, and some depression, among other health problems. He often went to Menton, France, to recuperate and rest. He preached his final sermon at the Metropolitan Tabernacle on June 7, 1891, and died in France on January 31, 1892, at the age of fifty-seven. He was buried in Norwood Cemetery in London.

Charles Haddon Spurgeon lived a life devoted to God. His sermons and writings continue to influence Christians all over the world.

# Other Similar Titles

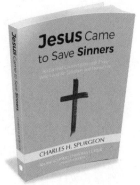

## *Jesus Came to Save Sinners,*
## by Charles H. Spurgeon

This is a heart-level conversation with you, the reader. Every excuse, reason, and roadblock for not coming to Christ is examined and duly dealt with. If you think you may be too bad, or if perhaps you really are bad and you sin either openly or behind closed doors, you will discover that life in Christ is for you too. You can reject the message of salvation by faith, or you can choose to live a life of sin after professing faith in Christ, but you cannot change the truth as it is, either for yourself or for others. As such, it behooves you and your family to embrace truth, claim it for your own, and be genuinely set free for now and eternity. Come and embrace this free gift of God, and live a victorious life for Him.

*Available where books are sold.*

### *According to Promise,*
### by Charles H. Spurgeon

The first part of this book is meant to be a sieve to separate the chaff from the wheat. Use it on your own soul. It may be the most profitable and beneficial work you have ever done. He who looked into his accounts and found that his business was losing money was saved from bankruptcy.

The second part of this book examines God's promises to His children. The promises of God not only exceed all precedent, but they also exceed all imitation. No one has been able to compete with God in the language of liberality. The promises of God are as much above all other promises as the heavens are above the earth.

*Available where books are sold.*

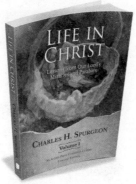

*Life in Christ (Vol. 1),*
by Charles H. Spurgeon

Men who were led by the hand or groped their way along the wall to reach Jesus were touched by his finger and went home without a guide, rejoicing that Jesus Christ had opened their eyes. Jesus is still able to perform such miracles. And, with the power of the Holy Spirit, his Word will be expounded and we'll watch for the signs to follow, expecting to see them at once. Why shouldn't those who read this be blessed with the light of heaven? This is my heart's inmost desire.

– Charles H. Spurgeon

*Available where books are sold.*

*The Soul Winner,* by Charles H. Spurgeon

As Christians, our main business is to win souls. But, in
Spurgeon's own words, "like shoeing-smiths, we need to know
a great many things. Just as the smith must know about horses
and how to make shoes for them, so we must know about souls
and how to win them for Christ." Learn about souls, and how
to win them, from one of the most acclaimed soul winners of
all time.

*Available where books are sold.*

*Come Ye Children,* by Charles H. Spurgeon

Teaching children things of the Lord is an honor and a high calling. Children have boundless energy and may appear distracted, but they are capable of understanding biblical truths even adults have a hard time grasping. Children's minds are easily impressed with new thoughts, whether good or bad, and will remember many of their young lessons for the rest of their life. Adults and churches tend to provide entertainment to occupy the children, but children ought to have our undivided attention. Jesus said, let the little children come to me. They were worthy of His time and devotion, and they are worthy of ours.

*Available where books are sold.*